Adventures of Ms. Kelly in Tallahassee

BY
CALVIN DIRICKSON

Order this book online at www.trafford.com
or email orders@trafford.com

Most Trafford titles are also available at major online book retailers.

Note for Librarians: A cataloguing record for this book is available from Library
and Archives Canada at www.collectionscanada.ca/amicus/index-e.html

Printed in Victoria, BC, Canada.

ISBN: 978-1-4251-5329-8 (sc)
ISBN: 978-1-4251-8404-9 (hc)

*Our mission is to efficiently provide the world's finest, most comprehensive
book publishing service, enabling every author to experience success.
To find out how to publish your book, your way, and have it available
worldwide, visit us online at www.trafford.com/*

Trafford rev. 10/2/09

 www.trafford.com

North America & international
toll-free: 1 888 232 4444 (USA & Canada)
phone: 250 383 6864 ♦ fax: 812 355 4082

Ms Kelly has a white body, Apricot ears and is a registered Apricot Poodle in her real life. I purchased her from a puppy mill; she wrapped her front legs around my neck and held on for dear life, as she explained in this book.

I lived on the four acre farm five miles south of Tallahassee and 20 miles from the Gulf Coast at Panacea.

It is true that there were two stray cats that appeared at my house and claimed the side porch as their territory. When I took Lin, one of the stray cats to the vet she did get loose in the Vet's office and it took the whole staff to chase her down, what a hoot that was.

The story about the blue racer snake and raccoon is true.

Ms Kelly did indeed outrun Red who was more than twice her size. I was an eye witness several times to that feat.

Ms Kelly was truthful about the, geese, peacocks, chickens, guinea fowl, pigeons, doves, Red, Suzie and her large litters of puppies, John Henry, baby bear, deer and the coyote that ran after the chicken in the front yard.

My house did burn exactly as Ms Kelly said and we moved to Miami shortly after the fire destroyed it.

THERE IS MORE TRUTH THAN FICTION IN MS KELLY'S ADVENTURES IN TALLAHASSEE.

ACKNOWLEDGEMENT

My first acknowledgement has to be for Mr. William Greenfield.

He is the greatest and handsomest friend I have ever had. He painted my picture for the cover of this book and sketched my picture for my title page. So everyone that buys my book will receive a signed copy of an original painting and a copy of an original pencil sketch of me. .

William took first place and honorable mention at his first showing in an art show in Bullhead City, Arizona.

BILL AND ME

Patricia Difurio is a great and dear friend. She encouraged Calvin to let me do the talking in my book. I have spent many nights with Pat, I have my own pillow on her bed and she gives me the best dog treats that I have ever eaten.

Mary Kontz is a great friend of my master and William Greenfield. I credit her for my book being published so quickly. Marna Musicant is another great friend. She let me play with her cats. Calvin and I visited her many times when she lived in Florida. She now resides in Philadelphia, Pennsylvania.

TABLE OF CONTENTS

Adventures of Ms. Kelly in Tallahassee

BY
CALVIN DIRICKSON

CHAPTER ONE

Sea Breese, a registered Toy Apricot Poodle, was in her final stage of labor and expecting to deliver five puppies before the day was over. This was a routine delivery since this would be her fourth litter. That didn't make any difference to the Henderson family; they provided her with the best veterinarian service money could buy.

Sea Breese and her mate Double D are the fifth generation of an exceptional family of show dogs. Their rich apricot color and perfect body shape, has made them the top winners for the last four years in the National Dog Show Circuit. These two alone, during their lifetime, have winnings of over $100,000 and still have a couple more years before retirement. These new puppies, as soon as they are born, will be worth at least $5,000 each—if their body structure is perfectly shaped and they have the deep dark apricot color like their parents.

The first one born was a girl. "I can't believe this!" Tommy, the vet, said to his assistant as he was looking at the new arrival with disgust written all over his face. "Go ask Margie if she wants to keep this one or have it destroyed."

Linda, the vet assistant left the operating room in a hurry. She being an animal lover was not about to ask Margie if she wanted the puppy destroyed, just because it was born with a white body and is a full blooded Toy Apricot Poodle. She knew that Margie, being the manager for the Henderson family show dogs and also owner of this puppy farm, was in the dog business to make the biggest profit possible. She would surely want to destroy any animal that would not make her money.

When Linda found Margie she said, "The first one was born with a white body. Only her ears are the deep apricot color. This color disfigurement has happened before in toy poodles but usually by the time the puppy is weaned the body hair will change to the correct color for its breed." Linda explained. "The vet asked me to tell you he believes she will be OK."— This wasn't a fib; since Linda was only referring to the fact that she was born alive and healthy. Linda knew it to be true that one birth out of a million or so puppies, the body hair would change colors by the time it is weaned.

"That's alright, we will keep her," Margie replied with dollar signs dancing in her head.

When Linda returned to the delivery room, Sea Breeze had given birth to three more puppies. All of them males with the dark apricot color and show quality built. They would easily be worth the $5,000 each, that one of the Henderson's dog handlers predicted.—But the little white female would be worthless and if the word got out that Sea Breeze had this off color puppy it would lower the value of all four litters she had produced.

By the time I was eight weeks old my mother told me this story many times. She explained this was how I was born and that Linda had saved my life. I wish someone could save me from my mean brother's teasing and ridicule. I still have my white body and will have it the rest of my life and that is enough for my mean brothers to tease me unmercifully.

"You are the ugliest Apricot Poodle that I have ever set my eyes on," my brothers are always telling me. They would say, "You look like an albino, except for your apricot ears."

They have made everyday of my short life miserable. I am now three months old and I overheard one of the Henderson's family supervisor tell Margie, "you have to get that white poodle sold soon,—or else." I took the "Or else," to mean I was to be destroyed.

My dad, the famous Double D, has been entered in dog shows for five years and has won Best of Breed three times. The last two years he has taken the top honors of Best of Show. Dad has such a beautiful dark Apricot coat with shinny curly hair. His perfect body structure, firm jaw line and fancy prancing ability is a trade mark of the Henderson's dogs. He is their most valuable asset.

Sea Breeze, my mother, a dark apricot, good looking dog, like dad she has been a winner in the show ring several times. The Henderson family took her off the show circuit early in her life to produce more show quality dogs.

My three brothers have perfectly shaped bodies and a rich apricot color just like dad. Jim is a dark color; Tim is lighter with long eyelashes; Larry has dark straight hair and a muscular frame; Ben the smallest has light curly hair and a barrel of energy. They are all highly prospective show dogs and the mean little brats love to brag about it.

My white body, bright apricot ears and slim build is the laughing stock of this puppy mill. I usually hide in the back corner of our small pen, depressed and lonely. Margie lets all the puppies out for a couple hours each day to run and play in a large open area. I stay in our pen because my brothers have encouraged other puppies to tease me about my odd colors.

I can hardly wait until we get a little older and just maybe my brothers will be taken away to be trained for the dog show circuit—and maybe then I could get some self esteem and feel better about myself.

My mother and father are always bragging on me about everything, except being a cute apricot poodle. I know they love me but I also know I was born differently then all other Apricot Poodles and I can forget about winning any awards or being famous, I will be confined to a life of 'Plain Jane,'—if the Henderson family allows me to live.

This kennel is mostly for raising and training dogs to be entered in the National Dog Show events. It is well known nationwide. To me it is just a horrible, crowded and ugly puppy mill. There are always misfit dogs like me that have bad markings that will be sold as pets,—if they are lucky. The only chance for me to escape a short life in this pen is to be one of the lucky ones to get picked as a pet.

I am nearly five months old now and my chances of getting adopted by anyone is getting mighty slim, I am afraid my time is about to run out. Most everyone who is looking for a pet wants a younger pup, one that is just weaned from its mother. Every time someone comes around looking for a pet my three brothers get in front of the pen to hide me. They are so ashamed they don't want anybody to see me. When people come looking for show quality puppies Margie hides me in a closet so no one will know that my daddy, being a popular and well known award winning show dog could have a daughter like me. It really hurts every time she comes and gets me; I know I will be put in the closet for the rest of the day and laughed at by every puppy that sees me being hidden away.

But today I am so happy my daddy has taken a break from the show ring and his owner brought him back to visit. My brothers were up to their old tricks trying to hide me and kept harassing me about my looks. Jim, the rat, kept saying, "You are so ugly it looks like you have been beaten with an ugly stick, or was it a stinky ugly fish that you were beaten with?" My other three brothers were rolling, laughing and kept repeating, "Ugly, ugly, ugly, little sister you are the ugliest of ugly."

"We know how you can get into show business," Jim said, "You can join a traveling carnival as a freak of nature." Again they were rolling and laughing so hard their sides were hurting.

I know I am not nearly as ugly as my brothers' say I am, but it still really hurts when the smart alecks tease me. Dad heard their brutal teasing and he nipped all of them on their rumps and told them to be quiet and get back in the corner of our pen. Then he came over where I was hiding.

"Honey," he said, "Don't let your brothers bother you, I know you have a lot of talent that those mugs don't have. You are beautiful to me and anyone that is looking for a house pet will love your personality, honesty and wisdom. You are much more advanced in intelligence than any of your brothers. Why you can already understand much more of the human and other animal's languages than even I can! I have spent many an hour in training on how to walk and prance across the show floor, and that means having a working knowledge of the human language. Your ornery brothers beauty is only skin deep. Your beauty is from within and shines much brighter than their sleek apricot coats. You will find the right person who really needs and wants a pet to love and you'll have a much better and fulfilling life than your brothers will have as show dogs. Have faith in yourself and ignore their nasty comments, I predict you will go a long ways in this world, much further than they will."

Dad really picked my spirits up and he is right; I know the human language very well. Most dogs only know a limited amount of it and I can understand everything they say. I know I am much smarter than any of my dumb brothers, but when they gang up on me with their teasing and their insults; it really makes me feel ugly.

It has been a couple weeks since dad's visit. Jim and Tim have new homes and will join other poodles in training for the show circuit. At least they are gone and no one can hide me when people come around looking for a pet.

My dad told me that I would find the right person for me, I just saw a man walking around looking at all the puppies. I overheard him telling Margie that he'd been a single father, his children are now grown and he wants a house pet to keep him company. My problem is that he is only looking for just one kind of dog: a Chihuahua and Toy Poodle mix (ChiPoo). These guys have the hair of a poodle that won't shed in the house and the aggressiveness of the chihuahua that will alert their owner if someone comes up to the house. This man seemed like a true animal lover and I liked him at first sight. This is my only good chance. I don't care what kind of pet he is looking for, I'm determined to catch his attention. I have just got to get out of this place before I go crazy or the, "Or

Else," that was promised will happen to me if I don't find a home.

By observing Margie when she unlocks the latch to our pen, I've learned how to open our pen door. Mother was sleeping; so I eased the door open and ran up to the guy as fast as I could. I began jumping on his leg to get his attention. He looked down at me and said, "Oh what a cute little poodle." Wow! He said I was cute. No one had ever told me that before. This is my best chance. I must do everything I can to impress him.

"She is a registered Toy Poodle," Margie replied sternly, "And I don't want to sell her."

I can't believe what Margie said. I know she has been desperately trying to find a buyer so she can get rid of me before the Henderson family makes the decision to destroy me. If that comes about she will loose money and knowing Margie she will do anything to keep from losing money on a dog. Yesterday, I overheard Margie talking to a friend and she said, "I've got two large standard poodles that are getting up in years and I just have to get rid of them so I lowered the price on them." Now she is putting those standard poodles ahead of me. She is about to sacrifice my life so she can make an extra dime from those standard poodles. How greedy can a human get?

I was devastated. I thought for sure this was the guy for me, now I don't have a chance to impress him. Looks like I am doomed.

I was so down hearted, depressed, ready to give up and crawl back to my cage. Than I remembered what dad had said, "Have faith in yourself." His words of wisdom gave me the strength to continue my quest. I had to think fast and do something quick before they walked away. I kept jumping on his leg, started whining, yelping and generally trying my best to get him to understand what I wanted. Finally, after many jumps, whines and yelps he looked back down, bent over and picked me up. I immediately wrapped my front legs around his neck and was not about to let loose. I licked his cheek for good measure. After all; I was in a desperate fight for my freedom and if not adopted soon, my life.

He carried me around in his arms, rubbing my back as he toured all the many dog pens. I kept my front legs tightly around his neck and I could feel an instant bonding between us, I desperately hoped that he was feeling the same. I kept saying to myself, "O please, please take me home with you. Save me, save me!"

We came to the end of the tour; I shut my eyes in anticipation that Margie would grab me and put me back in the small nasty pen. "Which one do you want, Calvin?" she asked. "I have two standard poodles that are really nice and I will sell them to you at a large discount." I thought to myself, "Calvin please, please, please, do not take her up on the offer."

I wish I could speak enough English to let him know that they are too big, old and ugly for a house pet.

"I think the standard size is too big for a house dog," Calvin replied as he kept looking at the pens full of small puppies. He stopped suddenly, looked down at me causing my heart to skip a beat as he pointed at me and said, "Margie, I will take this one right here."

"Oh what a wonderful day!" Finally someone thinks I am cute and wanted to take me home. I was so happy I kept jumping around in his arms until he almost dropped me.

"Margie, this little girl understands I have picked her. What a smart dog. I think I am going to have a great companion and pet," Calvin said excitedly.

Since Margie had lost out on her desperate attempt to sell him the standard poodles, she quickly said, "Ok, you can have her for $300."

Calvin reached for his wallet; and I knew that I was finally "Out of Here!"

He put me in the front seat of his van and started talking to me. Of course he didn't know that I could understand what he was saying. He patted me on my head and said, "You are so cute and I know you are going to like your new home. There will be no more pens for you I promise you that." I was having a hard time believing what was happening. He picked me out of a crowd of over one hundred small dogs as ugly as I am. What a lucky day for me.

I heard him tell Margie that he was from Tallahassee, Florida and lived about five miles out from the city limits on a small farm consisting of four acres. What kind of life and how many adventures await me in that city and on the small farm? —I wonder.

We buzzed around Tallahassee and turned on a black top road heading toward the coast. After traveling about five miles, we turned onto an old bumpy gravel road. Two miles of bumps then we turned onto a small dirt lane. After a couple curves we came to the end of the dirt lane in front of Calvin's house where there was a circular drive. Inside the circle was a set of railroad tracks about forty feet long. At the front of the tracks was a railroad crossing sign. Between the tracks and the house was a wooden fence the whole length of the tracks, covered with a thick growth of honeysuckles.

When Calvin parked and opened the van door there was a wonderful sweet smell from the honeysuckles. I love this place already. My new home is a wood framed house. The yard consist of two acres with a lot of shade trees, bushes and grass. The back two acres are mostly woods except for a one lane rutted road leading back to the National Forest. The house is an old farm house that was built about three feet off the ground. It has a wide front porch with stairs leading up to the floor of the porch on both ends. There is a carport on the left side and behind that I could see a satellite dish for the television. Ten feet to the left of the carport is the boundary line of the property. Like most farm houses it was built in the front corner of the property. The two acres of yard was mostly on the right side and behind the house.

On the right side of the house is a concrete patio. A large side porch takes up most of the floor space of the patio. Since the house was built so high off the ground, the side porch has eight steps from the patio to the porch. The porch has a built in area for the garbage can and several shelves with an open storage area near the roof. The door from the porch leads to the kitchen. The kitchen, living room and dining room are really just one large open room. A hallway toward the back of the house leads to a bathroom and small bedroom on the right. On the left is another bedroom and bath. At the end of the hall is a door to the master bedroom. After the master bedroom there is a door leading out to a very large screened-in back porch as wide as the house. Two doors from the back porch leads to the outside. One to the backyard and the other to the side of the house. On the right side of the house, about 10 feet from the side porch, is a grape arbor. The fence for the grapevines is 20 feet long and the vines are full of ripe juicy grapes.

There are several buildings on the far right side and in the back of the yard: including a deep well pump house, chicken house, two large storage sheds, a tool shed and a large enclosed bird pen 40 feet long and 15 feet wide. One end of the pen is attached to an old barn. Behind the back two acres is a huge national forest.

"What a wonderful place this is," I thought to myself, "It's a long way from living in a small pen. I can run and play all over the two acres of yard."

As soon as we got out of the van and headed for the house. I faced a big problem. I had never climbed stairs and didn't know how to do it. I sat at the foot of the stairs whining to Calvin hoping he would understand the problem. He recognized what I wanted right away and picked up my front paws and sat them on the first step then picked up my back legs and did the same with them. Then he sat my front paws on the next step and it only took me less than a minute to learn how to climb the stairs.

"You sure are a fast learner," Calvin said to me as I ran up the stairs.

When we got in the house Calvin sat at the kitchen table looking at my registration papers. He studied them for a few minutes, looked down at me, studied my facial expression for a moment then said, "Your name is now Ms Kelly." I thought that was a really nice name, so I jumped on his leg and yelped until he picked me up and hugged me. He laughed and said, "Ms Kelly I know you understand what I am saying, I can't get over how smart you are."

The food is great. I never had soft food. The only kind that I have had during my short life was a bland kernel that was hard, dry and difficult to chew. What a wonderful lucky day for me. I love my new home and Calvin my new master is the greatest.

There is already a large red dog here and his name is Red. He is very handsome with his hair a deep wavy red color and he is more than twice my size. His broad chest, strong big feet and wide mouth makes him look very strong which indeed he is. His master was a friend of Calvin's and since she couldn't take care of him any longer she gave him to Calvin. Red and I became good friends and we are always outside playing in the yard. It is so great to get out and play with another dog. I hope I am never placed in a pen again.

Red told me he was a farm dog in his younger

years. He protected sheep from wolves and coyotes. Now he protects the geese, chickens, guinea fowl and peacocks that run loose in the yard.

There are two cats that had come to Calvin's house on the brink of starvation. Their names are Lin and Kim and they claimed the nice side porch as their territory. They told Red and me we were not allowed on their porch.

The cat's made the open space near the roof of the boxed-in area into their sleeping quarters. Since the cats claimed the porch as their private property they would sit at the top of the stairs leading up to their porch and dare either one of us to come up. They would say, "Come on up the stairs, you dumb ugly dogs, and feel the sting of our claws and sharp teeth." Then they would open their mouths wide, hiss and show us their long wicked teeth and sharp claws. We could walk under the porch and since the porch floor was slatted like a sundeck we could look up at them but did not dare go up the stairs. The sight of their teeth and claws was enough to keep us at bay.

The side porch is the easiest way to get in the house which leads to the kitchen. From the front and the back doors it's hard for me to get inside. I had to scratch and bark loud to alert Calvin that I wanted to come in the house. It was a hassle having to go all the way to the back or front door just because of those two mean spiteful cats.

Red told me that the cats had never been around humans and probably hated them for how their mother was abandoned. They were near death from hunger and had finally got up the courage to come in Calvin's yard. They were so wild Calvin had to take food out to the far edge of the front yard and leave it for them for several weeks before they would come up on the side porch to eat.

"They were born under a deserted mobile home," Red told me, "It was lucky their mother was able to raise them until they were weaned. After they were weaned she moved off and left them to fend for themselves. They turned into wild cats and were always on the brink of starvation. Because of their living conditions they have a bad attitude toward everyone and everything."

When Calvin finally got them in a cage and took them to the vet to be checked over Lin got loose in the vet's office and it took the whole staff to chase her down. Red said he had heard it from a neighbor's dog that was in the vet's office when it happened. He said, "It was a hoot. All the animals were laughing. None of them knew Lin was a wild cat and she didn't know a vet's office was there to help her." He added, "She kept screaming at all the animals that were laughing at her, "I'll get even with everyone of you dummies."

After all Calvin has done for them Lin still will not let Calvin get close to her. Kim likes and appreciates all Calvin's help and will at least let Calvin pet her and she would rub against his leg when he comes out on their porch.

So far they are afraid to go inside the house, I'm glad, I like it for just me and Calvin in the house. I can always jump up on his lap and get a tummy rub, my favorite.

At least Red and I rule the yard. When we catch the cats in the yard we run them back to their porch. Since they won't let us on their porch, we will not let them play in the yard.

There are chickens, geese, guinea fowl, peacocks on the farm, and in the covered large open pen, are doves wild and tame, and beautiful fantail pure white pigeons. The pigeons and doves love their home. They have room to fly and raise their babies and the pen protects them from hawks and snakes and they have the old barn to fly into to get out of the rain and cold weather.

Calvin built them a large stone bird bath and a bird water tank where fresh water would run in it constantly. Calvin liked to go into the pen sit and observe all the birds and their babies. He let me in with him and I got to know all of them. They like their life and all the good tasting food they want and plenty of fresh water to drink.

There are four doves. Their mother came from wild parents and their daddy was from brown ring necked tame parents. Those four were a different color then any of the other doves— wild or tame. I noticed that none of the other birds laughed or taunted them because they were different. I asked an old granddaddy male dove why no one laughed at them because of their odd colors. He said, "Child, we are all doves, wild or tame and the color makes no difference. We love each other as brothers and sisters."

I thought to myself, "Why aren't poodles like that?"

Red and I got along great with the chickens, geese, guinea fowl and peacocks but had problems with a rooster named Tuff Boy. He gave us fair warning not to get close to his hens. He had long wicked looking spurs so I heeded his warning and gave him and his hens a wide berth. When I wanted to talk to him or one of his hens I kept a good distance between us. Actually he wasn't as bad as he tried to make everybody believe. I knew he was a good bird deep down and after he learned Red and I were not there to harm him or his hens we became friends.

Tuff Boy told us about the other fowl running loose. "The guinea fowl rule over all the chickens, geese and peacocks. They are very aggressive and will not let any of us eat until their flock has finished. They are excellent watch birds. One of them will sit high in the top of a tree and stand guard for foxes, coyotes, hawks and large dogs. When the guard guinea gives a warning of a predator being near all the animals are alerted." Tuff Boy explained, "That is why we do not care if they eat first, Calvin always puts out enough food for everyone."

Tuff Boy is ruler over all the hens and young chickens. Being the leader he always has to be on guard against predators and ready to fight to the death if need be, to protect his hens. This is a big job. It takes a strong, responsible, intelligent and loyal rooster to be the flock leader.

There is also a pair of geese, the male is called Tom

and his mate is Joyce. The peacocks are named John and Tammy. The geese and peacocks have nests hidden in the woods. They told me how Red watched after their nest and stayed with them all night as they sat on their eggs. "There are many predators in the woods that would eat our eggs and attack us if they found our hidden nests. Red has saved our lives and eggs many times," Tom explained. When I met them they were anxiously waiting for their eggs to hatch. "It should be any day now," Tom said joyfully.

What a lucky break for me. I still bite my foot to make sure that I am not dreaming. Dad was correct when he said that I would have a much better life than my mean brothers. I miss mother but it was time for me to leave home anyway. This is a wonderful life, with all these friends that think I am just a normal dog with different colors of body hair.

I remember dad told me that I would find someone to love me. I know Calvin loves me and I have found a whole lot of different animals that thinks I'm great. Since I can understand the human language so well they consider me as a wise and trustworthy leader.

Calvin works as a Financial Aid Manager at Florida State University. He is at his job from 8 am to 5 pm. In his spare time he made me a doggie door out to the back porch and one from the back porch to the backyard. I can now go in without trying to enter through the 'mean cat' porch.

Since we live at the very end of the dirt lane there are never any cars that come all the way down to the house unless they come to visit Calvin or his only close neighbor, Raymond, who lives across the dirt lane from Calvin's house.

A couple times Calvin tried to take me for a ride in his van. I was scared to get in. I had only been in a car the onetime riding home from the puppy mill and that time I was deathly scared but would not let Calvin know. Most of the time on that trip, until we arrived in Tallahassee, I kept my eyes closed. This time he knew I was scared so he let me sit on his lap and he rolled down the window and I stuck my head out. Boy was it fun! Calvin was holding on to me and I had no fear of falling. With the wind in my face it was a wonderful ride. The first time he only drove to the end of the dirt lane and back. After that I was ready to take a ride anytime anywhere.

Calvin took me to his office at Florida State University. He showed me off to all his employees and co-workers. Everyone thought I was the cutest dog they had ever seen. This really made me feel good. I pranced around trying to look as cute as I possible could in front of everybody just to get their compliments.

After visiting his office we stopped at a fast food restaurant on the way home. Calvin bought me a hamburger. Wow! It was the best tasting thing I have ever eaten. It was so good and I was eating it so fast Calvin had to slow me down. All the way home I couldn't think of anything but that delicious hamburger.

Later that week, Lin and Kim started hollering, "Red there is a poisonous snake on our porch come and run him away." They climbed up on the roof of the house and kept calling for Red. Red and I went around the house to the side porch. Sure enough there was a large snake on the porch. He could stick his head high up in the air and turn it from one side to the other to threaten anyone or anything that might come near. I had never seen a snake like that. Red said he is a blue racer and was not poisonous. Since Lin and Kim were scared of the snake, we decided to have some fun with them.

"You mean cats have just lost your porch," Red hollered up to them. "Mr. Snake said he was going to take it over and you two are not allowed on it. If you want it back you will have to fight him for it." For once they had nothing to say. They were terrified of the snake thinking it was poisonous. They stayed on the hot roof until almost dark. Calvin heard them crying, got a ladder and helped them down. When they finally found out the snake was not poisonous and was long gone, Lin said, "You two watch out, we will get even with you for this. We will take our time and when you are not expecting it, Wham! We will get even." We were still rolling and laughing at them as they were threatening us.

Red and I were playing in the yard late in the afternoon when the geese and peacocks came prancing in with their new brood of babies. They had hatched the night before and were now strong enough to follow their parents up to the house.

"I will sleep in the chicken house with the new babies," Red announced. "Snakes, raccoons, coyotes and foxes would snatch them in a second if I am not on guard at all times. Go up to the house Tom and alert Calvin the babies are here. He will have to come out before dark to lock everyone up in the chicken house to help keep the predators away from the new babies."

The next day I was able to play with them. They were so cute and cuddly. They loved nibbling on my ears. It didn't hurt just tickled. Joyce and Tammy were so proud of their new broods. They sat under a shade tree all day and watched them play. John and Tom were standing guard while their new babies played and nibbled on grass. They are so full of life, investigating everything and tasting the different kinds of grass. I sat for hours watching them play.

When the goslings and baby peacocks were 4 weeks old they were feeding on the tender grass near the edge of the yard. All of us were distracted when we heard a loud boom coming from the National Forest. Someone had shot off a gun. Before we knew it, while we were looking toward the sound of the gun, a fox ran out and grabbed one of the goslings and headed toward the National Forest. Red, Tom, Joyce and I took off after the fox. Mr. Fox was not as fast as we were since the weight of the gosling slowed him down but he could cut sharp corners and would be hard to catch especially if he got into the thick bushes that were just ahead of him. In a desperate move, Tom and Joyce flew ahead of the fox and came down and attacked him from the front. When he stopped because of the geese attack it gave Red and me a chance to catch him from the back. He dropped the young gosling and ran into the thicket.

"My babies need food and I will be back," the fox hollered at us from his hiding place in the thick bushes.

"I'll share some of my dog food with you for your babies but will not allow you to take any of Calvin's animals." Red hollered out his reply.

The gosling was hurt and Red carried it back to the house. I went through the doggie door and alerted Calvin. He came out in the yard and took the wounded gosling in the house. I went in behind him and watched as he patched the baby up. He taped up his hurt foot and put medication on a couple deep bite punctures.

Calvin kept the gosling in the house for a week until he was healed and able to run and play again. When the gosling was returned to his parents he got a good lecture about feeding too close to the edge of the yard.

Red was true to his word. He had a half sack of dog food and he dragged it out to the thicket where we had last seen the fox and left it for him. We never knew if he got the food or not. "At least I kept my promise." Red said.

A while later, Calvin's father passed away and Calvin inherited his blue tick hound dog. She is very nice and her name is Suzie. She is tall as Red but not near as husky and she has the beautiful spotted blue haze color that is the marking of a pure blooded blue tick. Calvin's father was in the process of raising blue tick puppies when he passed away. Suzie was expecting babies in the near future. Suzie, Red and I spent a lot of time playing in the yard.

As time moved along, Suzie began to get bigger. Her babies were still not due for a while. She slept on the back screened porch and since she was getting so big it wasn't long until she was having a hard time climbing the steps up to the porch.

One evening I was sitting on the back porch with Suzie when she said, "I figure that my babies will be born before the night is over."

The next morning I jumped up and scooted out the doggie door to the back porch. Suzie was right, she was a new mother with a whole basket full of puppies 12 in all. Calvin came out when he heard them crying and gasped in surprise at the number of them. We sat there all morning long watching the new arrivals. The next day Calvin and I went to town and purchased some canned dog milk. One puppy was very small and he needed extra milk from a bottle. We called the little guy Pee Wee and it took him awhile to understand that the nipple on the bottle was for him to suck on. When he learned how to suck on the nipple he really went to town on it. Suzie had a lot of milk but Pee Wee being the runt of the litter would probably not have made it without the help from the bottle. In two weeks he was as big and feisty as the rest of his brothers and sisters.

The puppies were so cute. I stayed on the porch with Suzie every day and night the first two weeks of their lives. After that the babies had their eyes open and were walking and running all over the porch. I got so attached to them that it felt as if they were mine.

At four weeks old their teeth had come through, they were eating food and were big enough to play in the yard. There was so many of them that Calvin didn't try to name them. He figured when he found new homes for them their new owners could name them.

So we had a yard full of noisy boisterous puppies. Being registered blue ticks they were all the same color. They were so much fun to play with. But it didn't take long for me and Red to get worn out and would have to get away from them to rest awhile. What a sight, puppies were everywhere. It took both Suzie and Red to guard them against predators. There are hawks and coyotes that would snatch one if they got half a chance. At six weeks they began to talk, loved to wrestle and play fight. By the tenth week they were weaned and eating puppy food. Calvin began advertising and calling people to get them new homes. By the time they were three months old every puppy had a new home. He would interview the person that wanted a puppy and visit their home to make sure they had plenty of room to play. It was so quiet with all the puppies gone. I was hoping that Calvin would keep one of them but with three dogs and two cats I guess that was enough for one little farm.

Just a couple weeks after the puppies had new homes, three German Shepherd dogs belonging to a neighbor came down to stay with Suzie for a few days. Calvin took Suzie to the vet to have her spade so she couldn't have anymore puppies but he waited too long—Suzie was expecting again.

Calvin brought home a surprise. His name was

John Henry and he is a registered male Apricot Toy Poodle. John Henry came from a poor family and didn't know anything about show dogs. He thought I was very cute and didn't know that I was also a registered Apricot Toy Poodle and that my color should be the same as his.

Now there are four dogs at Calvin's home. Since there are four of us the cats are afraid if they give us a hard time we would take over the porch from them. It is nice to have the upper hand over those rotten mean cats for a change.

With Suzie being a hunting dog, we had to warn her not to bother any of Calvin's chickens, geese, guineas or peacocks. She did go out in the National Forest and hunt for rabbits and raccoons. John Henry, Red and me would go with her. It was dangerous for her to go alone. The coyotes would gang up on her if they caught her out by herself. Since there were four of us no animal in the woods attempted to bother us. They would watch from behind bushes but they were afraid to try and take us on.

Suzie started getting awful big again. John Henry, Red and I decided to bet how many puppies that Suzie would have and what day they would be born. The bet was a leather bone. Calvin would give us one bone each month to chew on, that was the bet and the one that won got all the bones for the next month. It looked to me like Suzie was bigger than the last time so I guessed 13 puppies and I guessed the arrival date to be the 13th of the next month.

As Suzie got larger she quit her hunting in the National Forest and as it got closer to the birth of her puppies she quit playing with us in the yard. When she climbed the stairs to the back porch I could hear her grunting and moaning. A week before her time she could not get up and down the stairs. Her babies were born on the 12th and there were 13 healthy babies. I had missed by one day but luckily guessed the correct number of puppies. I won all the bones for a month.

I felt sorry for the two guys and Suzie, so I said to them, "You all can keep your bones;" besides there was no way I could eat that many bones in a month as tiny as I am.

Since their daddy was a German Shepherd they all looked like him. They grew fast and by the time they were weaned they were almost as big as me. When they were four weeks old they were big enough to play in the yard but were already too rough for me to play with. I sat on the sideline and let them play fight each other. Suzie was so proud of her new babies she would sit under a shade tree all day and watch them play.

Suzie, Red, John Henry and me kept guard over them at all times. Several times we caught a coyote sitting at the edge of the woods with his mouth watering watching every move we made. We would all walk slowly toward him and let him know that he was not about to get any of the puppies.

Sometimes while watching the puppies, I would think it would be nice to have some babies of my own. Calvin was able to give all the puppies away by the time they were 10 weeks old. This time Calvin took Susie to the vet so there would not be anymore puppies from her. We visited every puppy's new home to make sure they were ok. Since they were half German Shepherd and looked like German Shepherds, most of them were in training to be guard dogs. They were all happy in their new homes and liked being watch dogs for their new masters.

The baby geese and peacocks were near grown and were big enough to fly. Calvin had a small kiddy pool for the young geese to swim in and for Tom and Joyce he had a larger adult pool. Sometimes Red and Suzie would go with Tom and Joyce to a large lake in the National Forest. They loved to swim in the lake and now their young ones could go with them. This was dangerous because it was deep in the National Forest, Red and Suzie had to stand guard while the geese took their swim. They said they didn't mind because it was fun to go in the forest. Red said that almost every time they went to the lake there were always some predators sitting in the brush just waiting for a chance to nab one of the young goslings.

I overheard Calvin talking to a lady friend and he said that he was planning on raising poodles to show when he retired. I thought to myself, "That was why he had purchased John Henry." I didn't want show dogs around me. It looked like my wonderful life was coming to an end. If there is to be a lot of dogs moving in, I would be laughed at and called the ugliest dog in the world again. I just don't understand show dogs. Why should they look down on dogs of multi—

colors? I became depressed about the situation. Playing in the yard with Red, Suzie and John Henry was not fun anymore. I mostly just stayed in the house or aggravated the cats. I was so afraid my good life was over. I got so depressed and sickly that Calvin took me to the vet. He couldn't figure out what was wrong with me and just gave Calvin vitamins to give me. I wish I could make Calvin understand what is really bothering me.

SUZIE'S FIRST LITTER AT FOUR WEEKS OLD.

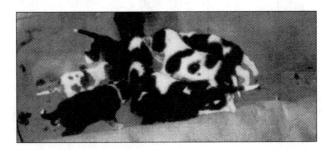

CHAPTER TWO

I was lying in my little bed a month after I heard the bad news about the puppy mill coming to Calvin's farm. I was still depressed and feeling awful when I overheard Calvin talking to his lady friend.

"I have changed my mind about raising and showing poodles," he said. "That would be more than a full-time job and I want to enjoy my retirement without any obligations." I was so happy I jumped for joy and ran and leaped in Calvin's lap, yelping and trying to lick his face. He told his friend, "She knows what I said. This little girl is the smartest dog I have ever had," he added as he picked me up and gave me a big hug. So I'm back to my happy life since the puppy mill was cancelled; enjoying myself and playing with Red, Suzie and John Henry.

It's early spring in Tallahassee and Calvin is busy

making a garden. Red said, "It's our job to keep the rabbits out of it. Calvin has a strong fence around the garden but they can dig underneath it. This will be a big night and day job." The rabbits would beg us to let them in to eat the delicious carrots and lettuce that Calvin was growing. Red would tell them, "No, you can eat all the good grass and clover that grows in the yard, Calvin planted that for you all to eat. The garden is for Calvin and his friends."

John Henry was bragging about using the side porch to get in the house. He said, while swaggering, prancing around and being silly with his chest sticking out. "I'm not afraid of those dumb ugly cats," he bragged while pacing back and forth at the foot of their stairs. "I am smarter and can run faster than any cat. Besides I have never met a cat I couldn't lick. I will easily get by them before they can attack." Lin was sitting at the top of the stairs. This was her guard post to protect their territory and she, being the meaner of the two, with the longest claws and sharpest teeth, hollered down to John Henry.

"Come on up John Henry I'll turn that beautiful apricot coat of yours into a blood splattered ugly one. I'll make you a deal. If you can get by me without getting clawed I will allow you to use the porch anytime you want. Come on and try your luck."

"That's a good deal I'll take you up on it," John Henry replied

He backed up off the patio, scratched the ground with his back feet, acted and sounded like a motorcycle, got a good running start at the stairs and was flying up them at top speed. But he wasn't near fast enough. Lin smacked him twice on the ears with her claws before you could blink an eye. John screamed out in pain and jumped back off the porch.

Lin and Kim were rolling around laughing at him.

"You are such a dumb dog thinking you could get past me," Lin said. "I am the fastest cat alive." John Henry was young and had never been around cats that would fight him. This was a good lesson for him. You never judge a book by its cover and if you are a small dog you don't mess with cats.

One warm sunny Saturday morning Calvin was out in the yard early. He was looking over and surveying the yard on the side of the house where Kim and Lin's porch stood. This was a large open level area, just past the grapevines. The grass was nice and thick, there were no trees or bushes to interfere with its growth. Calvin walked up to the front of the lawn and drove down a tall stake in the ground. Then he started walking toward the back of the open lawn and counting off his steps as he went. When he counted out 100 steps he put another stake in front of him and lined it up in a straight line with the first one and drove the second one into the ground as deep as the first one.

I was puzzled at what was taking place. "What was he building anyway?"

In a few minutes Raymond came over and they began talking about a dog race. Calvin called it a Mutt race and it was to be held the next month at the Greyhound Race Track in Monticello, Florida, a small town about twenty miles from Tallahassee.

After getting the second stake driven down they both stood back and admired Calvin's work. Raymond came over to where I was sitting and watching all the action, he bent over and picked me up. He carried me to the first stake that Calvin had anchored to the ground. Calvin went to the second stake and squatted down, looked at Raymond and he began calling me.

"Come on Ms Kelly run to me as fast as you can!" He called excitingly while clapping his hands. I started running toward him.

"Come on Ms Kelly run faster, come on faster, faster."

As I sped up, I thought to myself, "I'll show Calvin just how fast I can run." I kicked it into high gear and ran as fast as my little legs would carry me. When I got to Calvin I took a flying leap and landed in his arms.

Calvin said to me while patting me on the back, "Wow! Ms Kelly you sure are a fast runner for your size."

Even a dumb dog would know what building this runway and having me run as fast as I could from one to the other was for, I was to be entered in the Mutt race. I listened closely while Calvin was telling Raymond all the details about the race. It was open to all dogs except Greyhounds. There were several races and the dogs were separated into weight groups to make the race competitive. I would be running in the five to ten pound class since I weighed in at seven pounds. The more I heard and understood about the race the more excited I became about participating in it.

I knew, since I was a little tyke that I was a fast runner. I could easily outrun my brothers. That was the only thing that I was better at than they were. I was always challenging them to race, but after they knew I could easily outrun them, they would not race with me anymore

"I have got to put Ms Kelly on a strict diet. She can not have greasy hamburgers or fattening treats," Calvin declared.

"O NO"! "I can't have anymore delicious hamburgers or my favorite treats. This is going to be extremely hard to do," I said to myself.

The next day I was officially in training, I was to run half way to the end of the dirt lane and back, Calvin would ride his bike along with me for protection. The closer it came to the day of the race the more excited and nervous I became. A week before the race I could easily run the training course down and back on the dirt lane without even breathing heavy. On my last day of training, the day before the race I was feeling great, the only draw back, I was getting very nervous. That night Calvin gave me a doggie pill before we went to bed, that helped me get a good night sleep. Without it I know I would have been a nervous wreck and probably would have stayed awake all night.

On the day of the race, Calvin allowed Red, Suzie and John Henry to come along with me to help calm my nerves. We arrived at the track four hours before the race. Getting there that early gave me a chance to get familiar with the track and get to know all my competition. As I walked around the open area where I could talk to all the dogs that were entered in the races. I stopped where a small group of dogs was listening to a Cocker Spaniel named Billy Bob. He was bragging about how fast he was.

"I am the fastest and smartest dog here. None of you have a chance against me. I have won this race the last three years in a row. You all will just have to fight for second place," he said, with a boastful grin on his face

The owner of the track allowed some of the greyhounds to mingle with us. To give us pointers and answer any questions we may have about running in the race. Molly a dark brindle greyhound invited me to take a walk with her and we moved out of hearing range.

"Ms Kelly, I think you have a chance to take this race," Molly said. "I know you have never raced in an official mutt race before so I want to go over some fine points with you. First try your best to calm your nerves; everyone in the race is going to be nervous and that's normal, just do your best to stay calm. Next, and this is the most important thing to remember, pace yourself. Don't try and get to the lead until you get to the last turn. Just stay with the pack. The next most important thing is have faith in yourself. There are always one or two dogs that will brag on how fast they are and how you cannot possibly beat them. Don't listen to their propaganda. Those guys will usually burn up energy foolishly during a race and end up losing. When you are in a close race keep

44

saying, I can win, I can win."

I felt much better and my nerves had calmed down some after my walk and talk with Molly. I thanked her for all her help and said to her, "I know it will help me."

Before I knew it I was in the number 5 starting box, with the number 5 blanket on. The bell rang and we are off! I didn't get a good start and found myself the last dog in the race. "What have I got myself into," I thought to myself as I looked at the back end of the whole pack. Billy Bob rushed to the lead and he was looking back laughing and hollering at all the racers. What Molly said about the big mouth racers is true, he is wasting so much energy bragging. He may aggravate some and make them nervous, me I am going to focus on what Molly told me to do.

Going around the first turn I finally started easing up in the crowd, halfway to the second turn I was leading the pack. It looked like my training was paying off. I still had plenty of wind where some were already huffing and puffing and slowing down. Billy Bob was way in front. He looked back at me and said, "Well Ms Kelly you are looking to take second place I suppose." When we came to the last stretch I turned on my afterburners and eased up beside Billy Bob. He turned with a surprise and shocked look on his face as I was coming up even with him. "Little Miss Prissy," he said, "You will never beat me," then he sped up and was again ahead of me. I remembered what Molly said to do in a tight race, I started saying to myself over and over, "I can win, I can win." Hearing myself repeating those words gave me the extra strength I needed; I was able to move up beside of Billy Bob. We were only a couple feet from the finish line. I stretched my neck as far out as I could as we passed the finish line. By the time I was able to stop the announcer was already speaking and said, "Ladies and gentlemen it's a photo finish. It's too close to call. It will take the judges a few minutes to review the photos and declare the winner."

Waiting for the results made each minute seem like an hour. The crowd was getting impatient; they were holding their betting tickets squeezed tightly in their hands, waiting to find out if they won or lost their bets. Me, I was so nervous I could not look at the scoreboard I just laid down and shut my eyes, my favorite way to block everything out.

After about five minutes, which seemed like hours, there was a roar from the crowd. I opened my eyes and looked at the scoreboard and number 5 was declared the winner! It was me—I'd won by a nose! Calvin was jumping up and down and hollering at the top of his voice. "Ms Kelly!" He hollered proudly, "You won." He grabbed me up in his excitement and lifted me over his head and said, "What a great dog you are!"

Calvin was still full of excitement as he carried me proudly to the winner's circle. He received a beautiful trophy with my name already printed on it and a large check. I was so proud that I could do this for my master. If my brothers could only see me now I know they would be envious of my accomplishments.

On the way home everyone was excited and trying to talk at once. I still was numb and in a tizzy, I couldn't believe that I had actually won. When Calvin's van turned in on the dirt lane, animals were lined up on the side of the lane hollering and congratulating me on my win. I was surprised that the word had already gotten to the dirt lane. I was so high with excitement it took me a couple days to come back down to earth.

Calvin had a mobile home at the edge of the woods that he rented out. A new family moved in. They were a young couple, Ron and Mary and their two little girls, Nancy was just beginning to walk and Betty was about three years old.

Red, John Henry, Suzie and me decided it would be dangerous for the little girls to be out playing by themselves. There are rattlesnake in the woods. So we decided that when they were out playing we would hang around close to protect them.

Six months later the girls were playing at the edge of their mother's vegetable garden. Around the edge of the garden, weeds and brush had grown high and thick. I heard a rattling sound in the weeds; I asked Red what it was.

"That's the sound of a rattlesnake that has been disturbed and they are deadly poisonous," he replied. John Henry ran ahead of us and stuck his nose in the weeds trying to locate where the snake was. He yelped out in pain when the snake struck and sank his fangs into John Henry's cheek.

"Come on Ms Kelly," Red exclaimed, "Hurry we have to alert Calvin, John needs a vet and quickly." I got to the house first and began barking and scratching on the door. Calvin opened the door and I turned around and ran. Calvin didn't know what I wanted. I ran back toward him then turned and ran again, looking back at him and barked as loud as I could. He finally understood what I wanted and came running.

Red had returned to the garden's edge and bit the rattlesnake behind his head. When Calvin got there the rattlesnake was lying dead in the garden and John Henry's cheek was swelling. Calvin instantly realized what had happened and grabbed John up and took off running to the van. I followed him, hopped in and we took off at top speed with the horn blasting and the emergency lights on.

It was pure luck that the vet's office was only a few miles away. Calvin rushed John in and told the lady that this was an emergency. John Henry had been bitten by a rattlesnake. The lady took John Henry and rushed him into the emergency room. We waited and waited it seemed forever. Finally the vet came out. He had a sad look on his face, as he said, "I'm sorry but we lost him. The swelling got to his throat and cut of his air."

This was such a horrible day. John Henry had become a good friend. I couldn't believe he was gone. Calvin buried John Henry at the edge of a flower garden; he bought a small cross and placed it at the head of the grave. I was so upset over the death of John Henry that I would lay beside his grave during the day. It would take me a long time to get over my loss, but I am sure that John Henry is looking down at me from Doggie Heaven.

One day I was lying by John Henry's grave, about to go to sleep when a dirty mud covered, half starved dog came out of the weeds and tried to catch a hen. The hen ran squawking and flew to the top of the house. She started hollering, "Coyote, Coyote." All the chickens, geese, guineas and peacocks flew to the trees or to the roof of the house. There was chattering and noise everywhere. Tuff Boy hollered at me from the roof of the house, "Ms Kelly you better run. Coyotes like to eat little dogs." I looked at the animal again and realized that it wasn't a half starved dog but a big half starved coyote and he was coming at me full speed. I took off as fast as my little legs would carry me and was hollering, "Red, Help, Help!"

I could run fast but the coyote was faster and the next thing I knew he had me in his mouth. His teeth sank into me and I was in a lot of pain. I wiggled and squirmed but couldn't get out of his grip as he headed for the high weeds. The pain was so bad that everything was getting dark. Just before I blacked out I saw Red coming at full speed—I didn't remember anything else until I woke up in the vet's office.

"Ms Kelly has four deep and wide cuts from the coyotes teeth," I heard the vet tell Calvin, "But I think she will be ok. I've put in a lot of stitches in her cuts and had to give her a strong shot to keep down the infection and pain."

When we got back home everybody was asking me questions about my ordeal with the coyote. There wasn't a lot I could tell since I had blacked out. Tuff

Boy told me what had happened.

"Your weight in the coyote's mouth slowed him down just enough for Red to catch him." He added, "I never saw Red run so fast. He caught up with the coyote in a short time and bit his back leg. The coyote dropped you and limped off through the high weeds."

I turned to Red and said, "Thank you for saving my life."

After resting in the house for awhile I hobbled out in the yard. Tuff Boy came up and said, "Little girl, don't ever go near the weed patches, I know you are a little bigger than the puppies that the coyote was trying to get earlier, but you are not too big for a large male coyote. He will attack you in a second because they love dog meat. Also. keep a watchful eye on the sky, large hawks can also get you."

I thanked him and said, "I will watch anywhere for danger while playing outside."

This was a horrible experience but it taught me a good lesson, even though there is no danger of getting run over by a car there is danger lurking in the high weed patches. Tuff Boy has become a friend and helper.

Because of the near disaster with the coyote, Calvin brought out a hand weed cutter and I supervised the cutting of the weeds at the edge of the front yard adjoining the neighbor's wood lot. The weeds had grown up next to the barbwire fence separating the two properties. Now there was no cover for a coyote to sneak up and grab a chicken or me again, at least in the front yard.

Raymond helped in cutting the weeds. The wooded lot was next to his property and he had a house cat named Sally and he didn't want a coyote to get. I didn't know Sally at all. She was a house cat and only went out in the yard when she had to potty. She kept to herself and was strictly a stay-at-home cat. Lin and Kim would holler, laugh and call her Ms Prissy when she was outside. They were jealous of her since she had always had an easy life and never had to go hungry like they did when they were kittens. Sally had learned to ignore them.

It was a little before dark when I heard Lin and Kim hollering at Red to come help them. I ran out of the house and around to the side porch. Red was just sitting there looking at a wild animal on the side porch. The animal looked like it had a mask over it's eyes. Red said that it was a raccoon. The raccoon was eating Lin and Kim's food. They had run to the roof of the house scared to death of the raccoon. He had invaded their territory and there was nothing they could do about it.

They were begging Red to go on their porch and run the raccoon off.

"But I am not allowed on your porch, "Red replied. This is your problem that you have to solve." We sat and teasing the cats as the raccoon ate all their food. We would holler up to them and say, "Looks like you not only lost your food but you have lost your porch. Are you going to make your new home on the roof?"

"It's no big deal," Red said. "Calvin will give them more food. Maybe one of these days they will learn that we as farm animals need to work together and not keep up this silly feud or claim certain territories as private property."

Calvin was at work when two dirty looking men knocked on the door. I ran out the back doggie door and around the house to see what they were doing. One had a scar across his cheek and the other had a long scraggy beard and both had a strong odor like they hadn't bathed in years. When they realized no one was home they turned and walked up close to me, looked down and said, "Hi little pooch." All at once there was a net thrown over me and I was tangled in it and could not get loose. I yelled for Red to help me. Red came around the house at top speed. They grabbed me up and jumped in the car a second before Red got to them. I wiggled, squirmed, growled and showed my teeth, but they just laughed and ignored me. They put me in a very small cage in the back seat of their old jalopy. The cage was so small I couldn't turn around. They tore down the dirt lane as fast as their old jalopy would go.

I could see a little through the window and realized that we did not go toward the highway. When they got to the end of the dirt lane they turned the other way on the gravel road. We traveled several miles before they turned onto another dirt road and into a large forest. I'm sure that we are in the National Forest. We traveled a few miles in the forest then stopped in front of a rundown log cabin with an old barn a little ways behind it. I was taken to the backyard where there was an old weather beaten shed with a small pen that had a brand new fence attached. In the pen were 15 small dogs and I was dumped in the middle of them.

The dogs were sad, depressed and some were crying. They had been snatched from good homes and brought here just like me. One, named Rodney, could understand enough human language to know that we were to be shipped to Miami Florida to be sold.

When Calvin was talking about raising show dogs I had overheard him talking about Miami and that it was 500 miles away. If this was true and I was taken that far away, I would have to try and remember which direction that they traveled. I knew it would be hard to remember but I would try anything to get back to Calvin and the good life that I had grown accustomed too.

I started looking for a way to escape. The lock was a simple one and would be easy for me to open. The only thing it was too high for me to reach. Others had tried to dig out but the land was full of large sharp rocks that made it impossible. Things began to look hopeless. Most of the others walked the fence constantly looking for anyway to get out. Some would get so desperate that they would take their teeth and pull at the fence and dig until they hit a sharp rock and their paw would start bleeding. I tried to tell them that I would figure someway for us to get out, even though I was sure there was no way to escape. It would at least give them hope.

It looked like the two stinky guys had made this pen escape proof. The next morning Stinky and Scar Face came out and threw some hard dry dog food on the ground inside the pen. It had rained the night before and the food was muddy and dirty. Some were eating it since they had been here so long they were about to starve. I was not that hungry yet.

I overheard Scar Face say, "As soon as we pick up five more dogs it will make us a good load and we can head south to Miami. We got some good ones this time. They should bring a lot of money." He continued by saying, "I called Blackie and told him what breeds we had picked up. He will have new names and forged registration papers ready when we get to Miami."

It had been five days since I was captured. Finally I got so hungry that I cleaned off some of the food and ate it. It tasted awful but I knew I had to keep up my strength. I still had no idea how we were going to get out of this place. I even tried climbing the fence to get to the lock but I fell twice and decided that was not a good idea. I could get seriously hurt, then these bad guys would probably shoot me if I was crippled and they thought I was not worth taking to Miami.

All the dogs were getting desperate. They would cry and whimper all day long. It was so gloomy just sitting around waiting to be taken far away not knowing where we would go or where we would end up. Two days later they brought in four more small dogs, two poodles and two chihuahuas. They were very good looking dogs. They told me that they lived in the upper class section of Tallahassee and had wonderful homes. Their masters were rich and they had anything they wanted, tons of toys and the best food money could buy. They had all been caught while playing in their yards. Like me, they'd had a net thrown over them and rushed off in their old beat up jalopy before their owners knew what happened to them.

The next day they brought in a cute pug. He also had come from the upper class section of Tallahassee. He said that he had seen the two guys the day before near his yard as he was going back in his house. It was apparent that they were going to get him the same day that they got the chihuahuas and poodles but missed their chance.

"When they came back the second day they had a tasty treat for me," he said. "I got up close to them and they threw a net over me, grabbed me up and put me in their car in a small cage and took off." They obviously knew how to pick the most valuable dogs, except me that is. If they knew I was supposed to be a registered apricot they would probably throw me out of the pen.

The next morning we were to be loaded in cages and driven to Miami. We were all extremely depressed. It looked like there was no way out of our horrible situation. Most were crying and whining; they had such good homes since birth and had no idea how to take care of themselves. By being born in a puppy mill I had to learn everything to survive. I tried to help them by giving them some hope that we would escape before morning. It wasn't much and most of them had given up long ago on anyway to gain their freedom.

It was after midnight and I couldn't sleep knowing what would happen to me come morning. I would never see my good home or Calvin and all my animal friends again. My situation was very serious. I was getting desperate but could not see anyway out. My little brain had run out of all ideas for anyway to escape. I finally faced reality there was just no way out. Suddenly, I heard a voice from outside the pen. Someone was whispering, it sound like someone was calling my name.

"Is there someone out there?" I asked. I heard the voice again and this time I could make out what was said, the voice in the dark said.

"Ms Kelly are you in there?" I couldn't believe my ears. It sounded like Red. I ran up to the gate and he appeared out of the darkness, I jumped for joy. "How in the world did you find me?" I asked.

"Their old junkie car was leaking oil, Suzie has such a good hunting nose she was able to follow the trail of the leaking oil. We lost it when it turned into this National Forest. We have been searching the forest from one end to the other for several days and was about to give up when we spotted their old junk car. We can't dig you out, how can we get you free?" Red asked. I told him how to jump up and open the latch. He and Suzie kept leaping up and had moved the latch a little. All at once Scar Face came out the back door. Red and Suzie quickly ran behind the shed as Scar Face approached the fence.

He came out smoking a cigarette and was leaning over the gate. Suddenly he noticed that the latch had been moved and the gate was almost open. He froze,—with an alarmed look on his face, he quickly began looking around everywhere. After searching all around the cabin and barn he went back in the house and came out with a shotgun under his arm. He started walking around the yard again looking behind all the bushes and trees to see if anyone was there. With his gun pointed and ready to shoot, he slowly crept around behind the shed where Red and Suzie were hiding. I shut my eyes and held my breath knowing that he probably would find them and surely would shoot them. I kept listening, expecting that at any moment I would hear the noise of the gun going of.

After what seemed like an hour, he came from behind the shed and called out to his Stinky partner. Old Stinky came out and he told him he thought someone was in the woods trying to steal their stolen dogs. Scare Face told Stinky to stand watch for a couple hours and he would relieve him and stand watch until daylight.

It looked like my last chance to get away was fading fast. If they were going to stand guard all night there just was no way to get free. Stinky pulled a whiskey bottle out of his pocket and began drinking. We all watched every move that he was making. He started talking to himself and mumbled, "Why the heck do I have to baby sit a bunch of lousy mutts."

It wasn't long until Stinky was getting drunk and fell asleep. When he started snoring Red and Suzie came easing around from behind the shed. They had ran and hid in the woods when they saw Scar Face coming around the building where they were hiding. Stinky kept snoring and Red and Suzie started working on opening the door again. I cautioned all the dogs to be very quite and just maybe we could escape. Stinky rolled over and quit snoring.

Everyone froze in place, afraid he had woken up. It was so quiet I could hear myself breathe. It seemed forever. Everyone stayed frozen until Stinky started breathing heavy and snoring again. I told Red and Suzie to wait a few more minutes to make sure he was sound asleep. It took them a long time but they finally were able to get the gate open. I cautioned each one to keep quiet as they crept out of the pen.

We slowly slipped by sleeping Stinky and headed into the woods. We stopped at a dirt road quite a ways from the shack. "I know the way home," Red announced. "Everyone can come with us and I know Calvin will see that you all get home."

We started walking through the woods when suddenly we walked up on the den of a pair of foxes. They had four young ones about half grown. We didn't have to worry about then even though we were all small except Red and Suzie. They even wished us well and bid us good-bye, then added, "Hope to see you all again soon, one at a time," and give out a mean hungry laugh. As we passed their den, Red rubbed his scent on the entrance to show them who was boss. Red added, "Don't worry Mr. Fox if you come by the house I will always be on guard."

Next we walked up on a rattlesnake, which was guarding her eggs. Some of the eggs had already hatched. We gave them a wide berth and continued on. Red said that a baby rattlesnake was just as poisonous, if not more than an adult rattler.

After getting out of the National Forest we were able to talk, laugh, jump for glee and celebrate our release from that prison. Everyone was talking at the same time about things that had happened while they were dognapped and how happy they were to finally get free. It was several miles home and daylight was breaking as we staggered into the yard. I was never so glad and relieved in my life.

I ran through the doggie door and jumped in bed and landed on Calvin's belly. When he saw me he grabbed me and gave me a big hug with tears in his eyes said, "Ms. Kelly your home how wonderful. I read about the dognappers and knew that they had you."

Calvin called the County sheriff's office and Animal Control. Two deputies arrived and Animal Control was right behind them. It wasn't an hour later that the yard was full of cars. There were a lot of tears and joy as people came to claim their pets. Red, Suzie, and I sat under a shade tree watching everyone as they claimed their dogs. Every once in a while someone would come over where we were and pat Red and Suzie on the head and thank them for saving their pet.

I overheard the deputies telling Calvin that they probably would never catch the dognappers. Red reckoned he could show them where the cabin is, so I told him to go and pull on Calvin's pants leg then start walking down the dirt lane looking back at him.

I ran along with Red and kept barking and running back and forth. Calvin understood what I wanted and he told the deputies, "My dogs will take you to where they are hiding."

When we got back to the cabin, Calvin parked a little ways from the cabin, on top of a hill. We all sat in the car and had a bird's eye view of the cabin. One of the deputies knocked on the door and announced they were the police and to open the door. No one answered. He knocked again, still no answer. The deputy tried the door and it was unlocked so he opened the door and they went in. Nobody was home; Stinky and Scar Face had breakfast and it looked like they were in a hurry, they left the breakfast dishes dirty.

"Well it looks like they have high tailed it out of here." One of the deputies said as they came out of the shack and headed for their patrol car. They were getting ready to load up when one of them stopped—put out his hand and said, "Ssh—be still and listen." Everybody got quiet as a mouse and I could faintly hear a car coming through the woods. The deputies heard it too and drove their patrol car around to the back of the shack to hide it. A few minutes later the old rattle trap car pulled into the yard and Scar Face and Stinky got out. Before they could get away they were surrounded by the deputies.

In their old rattle trap car they had five pugs in small cages. They had already started their dognapping again. The deputies took them away in handcuffs. The five pugs were jumping for glee when the deputy took them out of the small cages and let them sit in the front seat of the patrol car. The deputies headed back to town with their two prisoners and the five happy pugs.

We headed back home so glad that this long ordeal was coming to an end. Stinky and Scar Face were taken to jail and three months later they had to go to trial. I heard Calvin on the phone talking to one of the families that had their dognapped. He said, "Well those dognappers will be in jail for the next five years. We won't have to worry about them anymore."

A month later Calvin began building a two room cabin in the front yard across from the house. I had to supervise this project. It took a long time since he worked on it only on the weekends. When he dug the deep and wide hole for the septic tank I stayed a way back. The deep hole scared me. I was afraid I would fall in. Finally everything was completed except the front porch. Calvin screened it in and put a doggie door in it so I could get on the porch and out of danger in an emergency.

Calvin rented the extra bedrooms to a couple of sisters, Brenda and Carol. They had two pug dogs named Mike and Joan. They could understand humans as good as me. They were ok but pretty fat and lazy. All they wanted to do was stay in the house. The only time they went outside was to potty. I didn't see much of them. I liked to play outside with Red and tease the cats.

It didn't take long until one day Mike and Joan, after they finished going to the potty, ran up the stairs on the side porch to get in the house and promptly got a smack from Lin for trying to use their porch. They ran back down the stairs with bloody noses and Lin gave them a sadistic witch laugh and said, "No dogs allowed on this porch." I felt sorry for them but I had warned them about the danger of trying to use the cat's porch.

Things was going along great, I made friends with all the farm animals except the cats. Tuff Boy would always let me know when danger was near. I had a couple close calls from hawks. If Tuff Boy had not warned me I probably would have been hawk food by now.

The two little girls, Joan and Betty were learning about the dangers and would always play in the closely mowed lawn. The incident with the rattlesnake taught them a good lesson. They loved to go in the bird pen when Calvin and I went in to feed, clean or just sit and watch them. Their mother was so glad that we watched out for her girls she was always giving us doggie treats.

I got to be friends with a couple of squirrels that lived in the trees in the chicken yard. They would come down and make themselves at home and eat corn that Calvin put out for the chickens. Tuff Boy, when he would catch them eating the chicken feed, would run them up a tree. They would get to a low limb and bark at him. They told me that this was their territory and until the trees produced ripe acorns and hickory nuts they had a right to any food in their area. They had a nest of new babies in a hollow limb in the top of one of the trees. The mother squirrel told me she had to have a lot to eat each day so she would have milk for her babies.

The squirrels also have a lot of enemies, snakes, hawks, fox and coyotes if they catch them on the ground. They told me this was the best place to live and raise their babies because if a predator comes around the chickens, or the guineas would usually see them first. When they sound their alarm they knew to head up to the top of the trees and hide. If they see them first they would bark a warning and the chickens, guineas, geese and peacocks would know to hide. That way they help each other. I learned all the animals' different calls when danger was approaching, this helped me stay safe.

Red and Suzie got so attached to Nancy and Betty that they were staying down at their trailer most of the time. Mary let them in the house and fed them food from the table. She thought both were the greatest watch dogs especially since Red had killed the rattlesnake that was about to attack her children. Mary was a big animal lover. She had several cats but they would never come outside, not even to potty. Mary furnished them with a litter box. I just don't know how any animal could spend their whole life inside a house.

A few times I got Mike and Joan to come outside to play, but most of the time they would just lay in the house and sleep. They are so afraid of the cats they will not help me tease them. I was getting bored, Calvin was gone all day working, Red and Suzie staying down at Mary's and the pugs were too fat and lazy to come out and play.

Calvin, his son Doug and I are off for a fishing trip, whatever that is. We are pulling a long wooden thing and Calvin is talking about putting it in water. I didn't think there was a puddle of water big enough for that thing. As we drove to the top of a small hill in the National Forest I couldn't believe my eyes. There was a puddle of water that went as far as I could see. When we got down to the giant puddle, they put this wooden thing that had seats in it into the water, I couldn't believe my eyes it stayed on top of the water! The only thing that I had ever seen stay on top were leaves from trees that fell in a puddle. I was learning so much; I over heard Calvin calling the big puddle a lake and we were riding in a boat.

Calvin and Doug were catching one fish after another. I didn't know fish grew so big and different colors. The only ones that I had ever seen were apricot in color, like my mean brothers and were in a small glass bowl at the puppy farm.

Looking over the side at the water while we were moving was lots of fun, until a snake swam up along side of the boat and stuck its tongue out at me. I jumped back so far I almost fell out on the other side. I climbed in Calvin's lap for protection and stayed there the rest of the day.

Red, Suzie and I were playing near the woods when I spotted an animal that was new to me. I ask Red what it was and he said it was a baby deer. It was lying still and looked like the ground with a brown body and lot of white spots. Red said that the mother deer had hidden her baby while she went to eat grass.

"Are deers good to eat?" Suzie asked.

"No!" Red and I exclaimed loudly at the same time.

The baby was always in danger of a coyote, eagles or large mean dogs getting it. I walked up and tried to smell the baby deer's scent, I sniffed and sniffed but could not smell anything. Red told me that a baby deer has no scent and that helped them survive predators. It just looked at me and I didn't know what it was trying to say. She smelled me and licked my face to let me know that she was friendly and that she knew I would not hurt her. I jumped around hoping she would play with me. She jumped up and was skipping around jumping over me and having a great time. I still couldn't understand the noise she was making but we were having fun.

Red joined our jumping and playing until I heard a strange sound and the mother deer came charging out of the brush. She had her head down trying to butt us. We took off toward the house at top speed, I looked back and since her baby was alright she gave up the chase.

Red said she thought we were going to hurt her baby and that was why she charged at us. He said that deer's hooves are very sharp and she would have cut us to pieces if we had not run to the house. It's amazing how quickly I am learning everything.

The pugs were very sad. They heard that Brenda and Carol were moving to another state and they would have to move with them. They loved it here where there was no traffic and no mean large dogs to bother them.

The pugs and I were outside and the cats heard about the move and was laughing and said, "Hey you ugly fat pugs we will miss you. Want to try and get on our porch one last time?" Lin said, "Please, come on and try it, I'll go back to the middle of the porch and give you a better chance. Remember if you can get by me you can come up on our porch anytime." Both cats as usual were getting a big laugh at the pug's expense.

The pugs ignored Lin and turned and walked away.

Lin started shouting as they walked away, "Cowards, cowards you pugs are fat little cowards.

Mike turned to me as they hustled away from the cats and said, "How do you stand those mean cats anyway." I told him to just ignore them and they will leave you alone.

The pugs, Suzie, Red and I were out in the yard for the last time before the pugs were to leave the next morning. I spotted the cats out in the yard in our territory. I told the pugs, "Come on you can get even with those mean cats by chasing them back to their porch and calling them cowards." Mike and Joan said at the same time, "O NO! We are afraid of them."

"Don't worry out here in the yard it's our territory and they are afraid of us." I commented.

I said again," Come on let's get them before they see us and run."

They kept saying, "No we are afraid of them."

Red whispered to me, "Lin is right they are little

cowards."

The next morning Brenda and Carol loaded up their station wagon and called Mike and Joan to load up it was time to go.

They all piled in and waved and hollered good-bye as they pulled out and headed down the dirt lane.

The cats hollered from the top of the house, "Good-bye you fat little cowards."

CHAPTER THREE

It was back to just me and Calvin in the house. He loves to lie on the couch and watch television. I liked to sit on his chest while he's watching. I could always get him to rub my tummy by grabbing his arm. Tummy rubs are my favorite and Calvin would do it a long time while watching television.

One day Kim surprised me and came creeping into the house. She had never been in the house before and was a little uncertain about being inside. Since Calvin did not make her go back outside I didn't either. I considered the inside of the house Calvin's territory.

It didn't take Kim long to get comfortable being in the house. The next thing I knew Kim had jumped up on the couch and was sitting on Calvin's chest.

"Hey little mutt," she said to me, "I get to come in the house and sit on Calvin's chest the same as you."

"You just don't try and get too close to Calvin's face, I am the only one that can do that." I nudged her back away from him and said, "If you scratch me Calvin will throw you out and will not let you come in anymore." I guess I made a believer out of her she moved back and laid on his stomach and gave me a dirty look.

I had to tolerate her in the house as long as Calvin let her in, but I would not tolerate her going out in the yard. I told her, "Don't even think about going out in the yard, that is still my territory." She always had to have the last word, she threatened, "I will sneak out there anytime I want and since I can run faster than you I will be out there every time your back is turned."

The next morning I was out in the yard and walked under Kim and Lin's porch. They started laughing hysterically and rolling around on their porch holding their stomachs. "Look at prissy Ms Kelly" said Lin pointing at me, "She now has apricot spots on her back. Maybe we should start calling her Ms Spotty." They continued by saying, "Hey Ms Kelly are you sure you don't have leprosy, it looks like it to us." Then they went into their hysterical laughing and rolling around on their porch.

I didn't know what they were talking about. I ran down to Mary's where Red and Suzie were. I scratched on the door and Mary let me in.

"What's on my back?" I asked Red. "Those mean cats said I had some ugly spots on me." Red looked me over and said, in a calm and soothing voice, "Ms

Kelly, it looks like where the vet sewed you up from the coyotes bite, there are four large patches on your back where the hair grew back. They are a deep dark apricot color just like your ears."

I couldn't believe it so I ran home and turned and twisted until I could see them in the mirror. Sure enough there they were, four dark apricot spots on my white coat. How awful! Now I am uglier than ever and Kim and Lin will have something else to tease me about. I feel as if the world is against me. First my mean brothers and now those two rotten cats.

I can recognize the sound of Calvin's van as soon as he turned in on the dirt lane, even before I could see it because of the curves in the lane. I would take off running toward him and he would stop as soon as I came into his sight and open the door for me to hop in. I got to stick my head out of the window and catch the breeze all the way back to the house.

The second time I went to meet him, I jumped to the open windows and I misjudged the distance and fell out and hit the ground hard. I got up dazed and stumbled around not know where I was. The next thing I knew Calvin was picking me up and checking me over for broken bones. I was ok, just knocked goofy for a few minutes. After that fall I was careful about jumping in the van and sticking my head out the window.

One day Suzie, Red and I were playing close to the woods when this large black animal came out of a thicket that was just inside the National Forest. He ran up to Red, licked his face, and turned to me and did the same thing, UGH! His breath was stinky, smelled like spoiled milk.

"He is a young bear," Red said, "and since our faces look a little like his he does not know that we are dogs."

The young bear wanted to play with us. He came out in the yard and was running and playing and seemed to be having a great time. He would give out a little growl as he jumped around and would run after us. We would run for a little while then turn and run after him. We all were having a great game of catch-me-if-you-can. He was too small to do much talking, just babbled baby talk. We had run and played for a good 30 minutes and had laid down to rest in the nice cool grass, when all at once there was a loud boom, the little bear's body jerked and he screamed out in pain.

Red jumped up and was looking down the small rutted dirt road that went through Calvin's woods to the National Forest. He exclaimed with a horrible look on his face, "Someone just shot the little bear!"

Calvin heard the shot and came running out of the house and up to where the little bear had fallen. He was bleeding badly. A man came out of the woods, with a long stick under his arm, grinning from ear to ear, his chest all pumped up and so proud of what he had just done.

"He has a gun," Red said. Calvin walked up to the man, stuck his finger up to his face and shouted at him.

"Get out of here! This is my land and I have 'No

Hunting' signs everywhere. Black Bears are protected. It's against the law to shoot them. I will report you to the authorities." The man turned and quickly headed back into the National Forest.

"What kind of gun was that? I've never seen one made like that," I asked Red

"That is a high powered rifle with a scope on it to aim better."

Calvin brought from the house some medication and bandages. He worked on the little bear for about 30 minutes. He had just gotten him bandaged up when we heard a loud roar and could hear something running toward us coming through the woods.

"That is the mother bear and she is mad, she thinks we were the ones that hurt her baby." Red said with fear in his voice.

We all took off at top speed for the house. Calvin opened the door and we rushed in just ahead of the mother bear. She started running around the house growling angrily and trying to find a way inside to get us. We all kept quiet hoping she would go away. She started scratching at the back door trying to break in. It looked like she would succeed in tearing the door down as one of her claws penetrated through it. I was so scared I hid under the bed and shut my eyes.

Calvin has a large shotgun he keeps for protection. He slipped out the side door and around the back of the house where the bear had been clawing at the door. The bear had come off the back porch and was checking her baby over in the backyard. Calvin fired two shots over her head. The loud noise from the shotgun going off scared her, she could see that her baby was not seriously hurt, she gave up the fight and headed back to the National Forest with her baby hobbling along beside her.

When the mother bear was running around the house Kim and Lin got so scared they climbed up on the roof. They were scared to come down and Calvin had to get a ladder to get them down. When they got down on the ground Red and I were laughing at them. Red asked, "Now who is the coward?"

"Come up on our porch and we will show you who the cowards are," they replied. And of course they had to add, "By the way Red who is that little doggie sitting by you with all those spots. Is that Ms Spotty?"

"Let me catch you in the yard and I will show you what Ms Spotty will do to you." I answered in the most menacing tone I could muster.

They just laughed and said, "Promises, Promises."

It's November and I overheard the news on Calvin's television, the weather man said. "There is a hurricane coming. It is out in the Gulf of Mexico wandering back and forth from Pensacola to Cedar Key." The next day the weather man announced, "This is the second day that the hurricane has wandered in the Gulf. She has finally made up her mind and is heading for Panacea and Tallahassee." Calvin and his son, Doug sat on the front porch watching the sky and waiting for the hurricane to strike. What I learned listening to the television weather man was that a hurricane is a very strong destructive wind with a lot of rain. I could see it on the television screen and the

73

announcer said, "This is a big storm and has almost completely covered the Gulf of Mexico."

I ran around the house and hollered at Red, "We need to warn everyone about the coming hurricane. I'll warn everyone here and you warn everyone on the dirt lane." I ran to the pen where the dove and pigeons were housed. I jumped on the door to get their attention and announced, "Listen to me everyone. There is a hurricane coming our way. I advise you to all go into the barn and stay there until it is over. The television announcer stated that hurricanes can kill animals and humans because of the strong wind and hard rain. Stay in your barn and don't come out until it is over."

I found Tuff Boy and told him to round up all the chickens and take them into the chicken house and stay there for the duration of the storm. Next I found the geese, guinea fowls and peacocks and explained to them, "Get to cover and stay there until the winds stops blowing. Under the house would be good shelter." Lin and Kim had heard me warning all the other animals and they climbed to the top of the house." I told them, "It dangerous up there and you will probably be safer on the side porch or under the house if you are afraid to stay on your porch." I went back to the front porch and sat with Calvin and Doug when the announcer said, "The hurricane has hit land at the outer islands and is heading for Panacea."

Thirty minutes later he announced, "It's in line to hit Tallahassee straight on. Then it will probably head for the Georgia line." He also explained that it had slowed down to ninety miles per hour after it had hit and pasted over the outer islands off the coast near Panacea.

About twenty minutes after it had hit Panacea it hit where we were. The trees were bending over almost double and the wind was howling something terrible. I got under Calvin's chair, this storm was really scaring me. Calvin and Doug did not seem to be in fear of it; they were laughing, talking and pointing at the trees as they were whipping in the wind.

Soon after the wind started the rain came. It was raining so hard and the wind blowing so bad that it looked like it was raining sideways. Now I was so scared I not only got under Calvin's chair but kept my eyes squeezed shut. Suddenly, after what seemed like an hour the wind and rain instantly stopped and it got very quiet—so quiet it was spooky.

I thought to myself, "Wonderful the storm is over and I can go out in the yard and play." I love to run through water puddles after a rain. Calvin and Doug did not leave the porch. They kept sitting there talking about the storm. I heard them talking about the eye of the storm. I jumped off the porch and began playing in the yard, running through puddles for about 30 minutes when suddenly the wind and rain came back with more force than before. As I went running for my life back to the front porch, already drenched from the sudden downpour, I realized what the eye of the storm meant. It was just half over and the second half would be worse than the first.

Later in the afternoon we lost our electricity, this

made it very scary. By night fall, it was dark as a lump of coal and the wind kept howling. I was glad when Calvin and Doug went back in the house and I ran ahead of them and went under the bed. Calvin had a kerosene lamp, which was the only light we had. Since the television would not work without electricity they stayed in the kitchen and listened to the news on a battery radio. All the stations were broadcasting information about the storm. Not long after we went in the house the wind suddenly stopped as fast as it had started. I came out from under the bed so happy that it was finally over—for real.

The next morning it was a calm and beautiful sunny day. Calvin and I got in the van and headed to Tallahassee. He turned on the radio and we listened to a weather announcer as he reported, "This is a warning do not come to Tallahassee. Many trees are down and roads are closed. There have been three tornadoes that came out of the hurricane and homes have been destroyed and trash is all over the streets along with the downed trees." Calvin continued on to Tallahassee ignoring the warning.

The radio announcer was right. The streets were full of downed trees and trash; we were not able to go very far into Tallahassee. Calvin gave up and we headed back home. The radio announcer said that we wouldn't have any electricity for a week. It was a good thing that Calvin had a gas cooking stove and a large freezer full of food. We were having steak for breakfast with our eggs, steak and french fries for lunch, and steak with baked potato for dinner. I had never eaten a steak in my life; they were as good as hamburgers.

The freezer kept everything frozen for a couple days. Then Calvin and I had to go to a small town that had their electricity back on and get bags of ice. This helped keep the freezer cold longer. After a week Calvin had to cook up the rest of the meat in the freezer and the animals on the dirt lane were invited for a feast. I got all the delicious hamburger meat that my little tummy could hold.

We not only lived at the end of the dirt lane but also lived at the end of the electric power that came from the Tallahassee power station. It was over two weeks before Calvin's power was turned on. The hurricane was very destructive for Tallahassee, even though Calvin's house was closer to the coast than Tallahassee, there was no damage to his house, buildings or trees on the four acres. All the animals wild and tame that lived on Calvin's little farm came through the storm safe and sound.

It's spring and I overheard Calvin talking to Raymond. After graduation at Florida State University, some students that have finished school and moving out of town would dump their pets out in the country. Our little dirt lane was an ideal place for animals to get dumped. The first poor little dog that got discarded by his owner came to the house on the verge of starving to death. His name was Tim and he told me what a good life he had up until his master graduated from Florida State. "My master studied a lot and was always home with me," Tim told me. "I got the best of care and had a big box of toys I really thought he loved me and that I would have a good home for the rest of my life. But after graduation he loaded up his car to move back to Texas, brought me out here, opened the car door and shoved me out and sped away, he dumped me like an old worn out rag. I was accustomed to being cared for all my life and didn't know how to take care of myself. I thought for sure I was going to starve to death. I was lucky to have stumbled upon Calvin's house."

Tim started crying, I felt so sorry for him. I can't understand some humans who want a pet to keep them company but don't realize it is a big responsibility and a lifetime commitment to care for them. Pets are so faithful and believe that they have a home for the rest of their lives and when they get discarded like this it really hurts. They need to have a class at Florida State to teach kids about the responsibility of caring for pets. Calvin took Tim in and even went to town and bought doggie vitamins to build his strength back up.

I liked Tim but he was a little too aggressive toward other dogs. I could tell he was part Chihuahua. His aggression was loud but he didn't mean anything by it, his bark was much worse than his bite. I teased him about his false aggressive action.

The word got out among all the animals that lived on or near the dirt lane. One of Calvin's neighbors, Donald had purchased two Pit Bulldogs, Samson and Big Guy. Those two dogs spread the word that no one had better even get close to their masters property.

They bragged that they had already killed three dogs before they came to the dirt lane to live and they claimed all the territory on the dirt lane as their property. They warned all animals that they would end up like the three dogs they claimed to have killed, if they dared to even step one paw on the dirt lane. Donald's house is not directly on the dirt lane only the side of his property joined it. He never uses the dirt lane since he has another road that he uses to access his property.

If any animal wanted to visit their neighbor they had to walk through the tall grass and woods. No one dared to get on the dirt lane. Those two dogs had everyone scared to do anything or go anywhere. Most would not get out of their yards; it was just too dangerous to go through the high weeds and woods, too many predators lurking in them. Everyone was a prisoner in their own homes and yard.

The first one to feel the wrath of those two pit bulls was Suzie. She had wondered down the dirt lane and was not near Donald's property. But just because she had the gall to get on their dirt lane they got after her. It was a good thing she could run faster than they could. When they first saw her they did surprise her, knocked her down and Samson bit a big gash along her side before she could get away from him.

Calvin heard Suzie screaming in pain and came running out of the house. When he saw what happened he was furious and called the County Animal Control. They came out and I overheard Calvin telling them that not only did the pit bulldogs attack and injure Suzie but they had also ran after another neighbor's children and would have attacked them except they made it into their house before the dogs caught them. Animal Control picked up Samson and Big Guy and took them away.

All the local animals were overjoyed and celebrated the seizure of the two vicious dogs. Now they could run up and down the dirt lane where most of them loved to play and visit their neighbors. Red, Suzie and I walked through the neighborhood and heard several horror stories about close calls from Samson and Big Guy.

Donald was very angry because the county had seized his dogs. A cat overheard him tell his wife he was going to get Calvin for having his dogs picked up.

When the pit bulldogs slashed Suzie, Calvin rushed her to the vet. It took 41 stitches to sew up her wounds. The vet gave her a shot for infection and pain, then told Calvin, "Since it is not a deep wound I think she will be ok."

The word came down that the county was not going to allow Donald to get his dogs back. The next day it was officially announced that they would keep them permanently. All the animals that lives on the dirt lane were dancing and celebrated the permanent seizure of the pit bulldogs. Their celebration and happy times did not last long. Donald appealed the ruling and the judge allowed him to have his dogs back as long as he kept them on a chain and behind a fence. All the local animals were very worried. They knew that pit bulldogs could easily break a chain and dig out from under a fence. It looked like all the animals on the dirt lane were going to be restricted to playing in their own yards again. Some were so afraid of the pit bulldogs that they would not leave their houses.

Three months after Samson and Big Guy returned, Samson broke his chain and dug out from under the fence. Exactly what all the animals on the dirt lane predicted. The first place he stopped was at the Jefferson's house. They lived back in the woods a little ways up a long driveway off the dirt lane. Samson ran down and killed two of the Jefferson's Persian cats. Next he came up in Calvin's yard. I was inside with Calvin as Tim went outside to potty. Calvin heard Tim screaming in pain. We rushed outside and Samson was standing over Tim laughing at him as he was dying. Calvin grabbed Samson collar and dragged him in the house and called the County Sheriff. I was shook-up and afraid with Samson being in the house. I couldn't believe that Calvin was brave enough to drag that vicious pit bulldog in the house. It was apparent that Samson knew that Calvin was so mad he had better not try anything with him.

When the deputies came they made a report of what happened. Calvin told them that the dogs had been seized once before but a judge let the owner have them back. The deputy called Animal Control to come and get Samson and Big Guy.

"Is it alright for me to bury my dog now?" Calvin asked the deputy, "Sure," The deputy replied. Suzie,

Red and I were lying at the deputy's feet taking in every word that was said. The deputy looked down at us and said, "Calvin I think those three dogs know what we are talking about."

"I am sure they do. Dogs and other animals are smarter than we give them credit for." Calvin replied.

When Kim and Lin heard about Samson killing the neighbor's two cats they ran up to their sleeping quarters on the porch and didn't come down for two days. We got to aggravate them again. Red and I asked them, "Why are you afraid of Samson? You said that you were never scared of any dog, could it be you are now afraid of dogs?"

They both replied in unison, "Just shut up and go play with Ms Spotty."

After Samson was taken away Donald came up the dirt lane and stopped at the edge of Calvin's property. Calvin told him, "Animal Control picked-up your dogs, they killed two cats and Tim and you are 'NOT' going to get them back."

"I wanted to see Tim," Donald said.

"I have already buried him," Calvin replied.

"Dig him up," Donald demanded.

"You go to Hell!" Calvin yelled back at him.

This was the first time that I had ever heard Calvin say a bad word.

Suzie came walking from around the house toward the dirt lane where Donald was standing. "I'll just take Suzie and shoot her," Donald threatened.

"I have a gun too," Calvin responded.

Donald took off running down the dirt lane like a scared Jack Rabbit, thinking that Calvin had said, "I will shoot you."

All the animals in the neighborhood had heard the commotion and snuck up where they could hear what was going on. When Donald took off down the dirt lane they were all rolling, laughing and hollering out, "What a coward."

A couple days later I overheard Calvin talking to a neighbor who thought Donald was a little bit crazy and was deadly scared of him. Calvin said to him, "I told you he was a coward. He beats up on his wife all the time and all wife beaters are afraid of another man. We won't have anymore problems out of him. I will personally see that he never get his dogs back again."

Red, Suzie and me visited everyone on the dirt lane. We told all the animals that this time the Pit Bulldogs will not be coming back. Several cats, at the same time exclaimed, "Are you sure?" I told them, "I am sure you will never be bothered with those two again." Calvin said that he would personally see that they never come back." All the cats were so happy. They were jumping around and singing, "**No more Samson, no more Big Guy, no more pit bulls la,la,la,la,thank you God, thank you God, the two devil dogs will never bother us again Mmmmm.**"

There are now a couple more houses on the dirt lane. Calvin and I traveled around to everyone and visited. I got to know all the new dogs and cats in the neighborhood. They were all nice and friendly. I don't know why we have the two meanest cats on the dirt lane. On one of my visits down the dirt lane, I was asked several times, "Why is Kim and Lin so mean and unsociable?" I couldn't give them an answer, the only thing I could say about it was, probably because of the tough time they had as babies. Dan, an old male cat said, "Just because they had a poor upbringing is no excuse for their being like they are." "I agree," was my reply. Things settled down after the pit bulldogs were gone.

We set up warning signals that we could send to each other if anytime there was danger lurking on the dirt lane, like wild animals or mean dogs. We all got along great and would play together. This is the way the world should be—no fighting just playing. If only Kim and Lin would ease up on their war with us.

Later that month Calvin had to go on a week's conference trip for Florida State and I was to stay in Tallahassee with one of his lady friends. Her name is Linda and she only had a small yard to play in. Linda has a Cocker Spaniel dog named Larry and a white cat named Snowball. They were not very pleased when I showed up. They were afraid I was there on a permanent basis. When I explained that I was to be a guest for a week they let out a sigh of relief. When I told them I was from a farm they had a thousand questions to ask. They had never seen or heard of chickens, geese, guinea fowl, peacocks or any of the many different kinds of birds that Calvin had in his large bird house. I spent most of the week telling them all about the farm, all the animals and the danger from predators. They were strictly city slickers: I had to explain to them what a predator was.

There wasn't much to do in town. They had toys to play with and that was about it. We were not allowed out of their small yard. I sure am glad that I live in the country where there are many things to do and places to go. When it was time to go home I was glad to go. Linda's yard was not much bigger than our family pen at the puppy mill and I felt like I had been teaching class for the whole week I spent there.

Two months later Larry and Snowball showed up at the house. Linda was scheduled to be out of town for a couple weeks so Calvin had volunteered to keep them. The first day that Larry and Snowball were outside, Lin and Kim had to show off in front of them. They told Snowball that since she ran around with ugly stinky dogs they would not let her on the side porch. I think they were a little jealous. Snowball is a beautiful cat. Her hair is long and soft like a Persian cat's, it was wavy, shiny and beautiful. Lin and Kim have rough ugly hair and a lot of scars from their hard life during their earlier years.

I told Larry and Snowball to always play in the middle of the yard. I said, "Don't go near the edges of the yard because you might get picked off by a fox or coyote and always pay attention to the other animals, especially the guinea fowl. They always have someone on watch for predators. Watch the sky, there are large hawks that would love a little dog or cat for lunch."

We had loads of fun the two weeks that Larry

and Snowball were visiting. Even Kim and Lin came around and would talk to Snow Ball sometimes. I was so scared they would get hurt not knowing anything about living in the country.

One day I was with them out in the yard playing and I let my guard down. Next thing I knew the guinea fowl that was on guard duty hollered, "Hawk, Hawk, look out! A hawk is circling above." When I looked up he was getting ready to dive and was heading for Snowball. She was close to the house so I hollered, "Snowball get under the house!" It was so close I shut my eyes knowing that she was probably a goner. I felt guilty it was my fault I wasn't watching enough. When I opened my eyes the hawk was on the ground with some of Snowballs hair clinging to his claw. He was stretching his neck and looking all around underneath the house. Snowball had made it; I don't know how, when a hawk goes into their dive it only takes them a second to reach their target. The hawk grumbled and mumbled. He was so mad that he had missed by a hair. He was still mumbling and grumbling as he flew away. He looked back at us and said, "I will get all of you one of these days. Each and everyone of you will someday be my lunch."

The baby geese and peacocks are now grown. The young male peacocks are very beautiful as they strut and try to make the sound of a grown peacock. The young males will be going to a new home. Calvin sold them to a zoo. The zoo had lost their old males and were happy to get the young ones.

Another stray cat showed up in Calvin's front yard.

It was nothing but skin and bones and looked like it had a rough life. Lin and Kim allowed it to come up on their porch. After checking the cat over and asking questions they found out that she was one of their sisters. When their mother deserted them she had gone down a different road than Lin and Kim and ended up at a house a mile away. The family took her in but when they moved they left her behind. When she got hungry she started looking for food and stumbled upon Calvin's house. It looks like we will have three mean cats to put up with. Lin and Kim named her Win. What a dumb name.

I soon found out that Win was much friendlier than Lin and Kim. She had lived with two dogs and they were all good friends. She would come down to the bottom of the stairs on the side porch and talk to Suzie, Red and me. She was very nice and we would let her run around the yard and play with us. Lin and Kim kept calling her a traitor. She told them that there is no reason to be in a feud, there is plenty of room for everyone. She asked, "Why do you two think the side porch belongs to you? I don't think Calvin gave you the authority to claim it as your own." She wasn't getting very far with her two mean sisters. They had hardened hearts from being mistreated so long.

Suzie, Red and me made a comment to Kim and Lin to at least try and get along. They didn't answer us but I could see a small crack in their hard shell of hate. A few days later we took one more step and we told them they could come out in the yard and we wouldn't bother them, as long as they were nice to all animals while they were in our territory.

It was Christmas day and Calvin's two children Kathy and Doug, who both were attending Florida State University, came out to visit for the holidays. It was an unusually warm day for Christmas the temperature was in the upper seventies. Calvin had purchased a billiard table for the front room and they were shooting pool. I was sitting in a chair watching the action. Even Red came in the house and was lying by the open front door.

After Calvin had permanently gotten rid of Donald's bulldogs he had said he was going to get even with Calvin. He owned a mobile home lot beside of Raymond's lot and he pulled in an old beat up mobile home on his lot and rented it out. I heard Calvin talking to Raymond, and he said, "They are rednecks and are having problems not only with me but all the other close neighbors." He added, "Donald only rented it to those rednecks to aggravate me."

I got tired of watching the pool game and wandered outside and sat down in the dirt lane enjoying the warm Christmas day. May Bell the wife of the redneck named Bubba came to the open door of their old mobile home. I was staring at her because Calvin said that they were rednecks and I was looking to see if I could find any red coloring in her neck. I couldn't see any red, not even small specks or a light shade of red on her neck. Where did Calvin get the idea that they had rednecks? I moved a little closer to the edge of the dirt lane. The sun was so bright and glaring on the old mobile home I wanted to get a closer look but after staring at her from every angle that I possible could, without getting in her yard, I still couldn't see any red coloring on her neck. I couldn't understand it, as hard as I was trying I could not see any trace of red on either her or her husband Bubba. I know I am not colored blind, maybe Calvin is.

May Bell didn't like it because I was staring at her and she hollered out, "Ms Kelly you better get out of my yard before I shoot you."

I was flabbergasted I was not in her yard. The end of the dirt lane was on Calvin's property. I jumped up ready to high tail it out of there if she came out with a gun.

Calvin just happened to be standing in his open door and heard what she said. "If you shoot Ms Kelly I'll shoot your ugly cat that is always in my yard." Calvin hollered back to her.

May Bell ran back in the house and I heard her tell a big lie to Bubba, she exclaimed hysterically! "Calvin said he was going to shoot me."

Kathy ran to the phone and Doug told her to dial 911.

Bubba came out of their mobile home with a long Japanese sword in his hand and started coming across the dirt lane. I kept backing up as he was walking swiftly toward me, making sure I was out of his reach. He was heading toward Calvin.

He got out to the middle of the dirt lane, Calvin was standing in the open door and pointed a finger at Bubba and said, in a loud clear voice, "I have a gun and if you don't stop and go back in your house I am going to drop you in your tracks." Bubba stopped and froze in his tracks with a surprised look on his face. After a minute of staring at Calvin he turned, mumbled to himself, and trotted back home. I had never seen Calvin that mad and believe he would have shot him if he kept coming with that long sword, especially since Calvin's children were in the house.

It was only a couple minutes when a county deputy's car came roaring up the dirt lane and came to a screeching stop at the end of it, in Calvin's yard. When he got out of the patrol car Bubba and May Bell ran out to meet him and both of them were trying to talk to him at the same time.

"I have to see Calvin first since the emergency call came from his house," he explained to them. When he got inside Calvin's house he shook his head and said, "They seem to be a couple of nuts." Calvin said, "I agree."

After hearing Calvin's side of the story he did go to Bubba's mobile home and told them that they had to get along with their neighbors, and he didn't want to come out again for an emergency call because of them.

That was the end of them trying to cause trouble and it was only a couple months later that Donald had to evict them because they were not paying their rent. I never did learn why Calvin said that they were rednecks. It was one mystery that I have never been able to solve.

CHAPTER FOUR

Calvin was getting ready to go to town and I jumped on his leg, whining and barking, my way of begging him to let me go. At first he said, "No Ms Kelly I am going on the other side of Tallahassee and on up into Georgia and it will be much too long of a ride for you." I started pouting and looked as sad and downhearted the best that I could. That wasn't working so I started all over again with much more acting in my pouting. Finally he said, "Ok Ms Kelly, you win." I jumped in the van so excited to get to take this long trip. Calvin said, "Got your way didn't you?" as he patted me on my head I tried to look as cute and innocent as I possibly could.

After letting me stick my head out while we were on the dirt lane we hit the gravel road then the black-top on our way to Tallahassee. We headed through the area of Tallahassee where I had never been before. It was interesting; I saw the state capital and parts of Florida State University that Calvin had never taken me to. Tallahassee is strictly a government/college town. We buzzed through town, crossed Interstate 10, came to open country and headed toward Georgia. This was all new to me. I'd never been all the way through Tallahassee let alone in the open country toward Georgia.

It was a nice summer day and I was enjoying all the scenery, seeing places that I had never seen before. I couldn't stick my head out the window but could sit on Calvin's lap and see everything through the window glass. It wasn't long until Calvin said to me, "We just crossed the border into Georgia, now you are an official Georgia gal."

We were still out in the wide open country when Calvin rounded a curve and a big truck was in our lane coming fast. It was heading straight for us, I didn't know what do and it was almost upon us.

I decided I would have a better chance of survival if I jumped down into the floor of the van. I hunkered down in the floor and closed my eyes tightly. I was afraid this was going to be the end of both of us. I can remember hearing squealing tires, a horrible scrapping sound and flying through the air, as Calvin's van collided with the truck. After that I didn't remember anything until I woke up and it was pitch dark; I was hurting all over and could taste blood. I moved my legs a little and decided there was nothing broken. I eased open one eye and a big black shadow was standing over me. I didn't know what it was so I shut my eyes again and decided to play dead. I held my breath and would only breathe shallow breaths—when I had to. I was expecting any minute to be on my way to doggie heaven where Tim and John Henry were.

This huge shadow kept standing over me; I could feel his presence and knew he was starring down at me. "Is it a coyote a bear or what?" My little brain was searching for an answer. I finally peeked out with one eye again and could make out a large black dog. I thought to myself, "I sure hope he is not like Samson or Big Guy." I shut my eyes again still afraid I was a goner.

"Little girl can you here me," said the shadow. "Are you alright?"

"GREAT!" He sounds friendly so I open my eyes and said, "I hurt all over and am sore. Can you tell me what happened?"

"Your master's van was hit by a big truck and he was taken away in an ambulance. You were thrown out here and neither the ambulance driver nor the highway patrolman knew that you were here in this tall weeds patch. Your master kept calling out, my dog Ms Kelly where is she? Please find her don't take me without her. He kept calling and calling your name and asked the patrolman to look for you. After they took your master away the patrolman started looking but he got an emergency call on his radio. There was another wreck for him to go to so he had to leave without finding you. I saw it all. I live just down the road and was standing over there near the woods when the accident happened. If you can walk you can come to my house. By the way my name is Joe and I take it that yours is Ms Kelly?" he asked.

"Yes, I am Ms Kelly, and I believe I can walk ok." I replied. I thanked him again for being here when I needed help. As we were walking to his house I was still in a daze. My brain would not function I needed to think about my situation and what I was going to do. I can't believe that my world fell apart so quickly.

Joe's master, Ben was very nice and took me in. Joe slept in a big barn. It was fun sleeping in the barn and smelling the fresh cut hay. This was a big farm with a lot of chickens, cows, hogs and horses. It was a nice place but I had to find a way to get back home. I know it's far away and I am going to have a hard time finding it. I don't know if Calvin is still alive, at home or in the hospital, but whatever the situation is I have got to go as soon as I heal up.

I heard Ben telling a neighbor that he had put an advertisement in the Tallahassee, and Atlanta papers about me. He was hoping to find my master so I could be reunited with him. This gave me hope that soon, I would make it home.

It has been over a month since the accident, I am feeling much better and most of the cuts and bruises have healed. There has been no response to the ad in the newspapers and I am afraid that Calvin was seriously hurt or maybe dead. I am so depressed; I have got to figure out the way home and soon.

A week later and I am completely over the accident. All the soreness is gone and it is time for me to head for home. No matter if Calvin is not there I must find out what happened to him. The next morning I got up early and told Joe good-bye and many thanks for all his help. He explained to me about the traffic and how dangerous it is. I had never walked on a highway before and I listened closely to all his warning, then I struck out for Tallahassee.

I had no problem knowing how to get to Tallahassee since we had traveled on only one highway after leaving there on our way to Georgia. The big problem would be finding my way back through Tallahassee and locating the road to home.

I walked along the edge of the highway shoulder close to the weed patches and woods, even though I knew it was awfully dangerous. I walked until dark but didn't see any lights for Tallahassee. I was very tired from my long walk and found a hollow log, a perfect place to spend the night in this dangerous wooded area. I crawled up in it for the night and I felt safe inside the log, so I dropped off to sleep quickly....
About midnight I woke up, I could smell and hear an animal just outside my log. I peeked out and by the light of the moon I could see that it was a coyote and he was less than 10 feet from me. I quickly crawled back in the log. He saw me and, came running fast and started digging at the mouth of my log. I scooted as far back inside the log as I could get. If he gets to me I would have the fight of my life. He had made the hole bigger and was so close that our noses were

almost touching.

He started singing, "*I'm going to have me a little dog for dinner, O yes, O yes, I'm going to have a good tasting tender young dogs. Little dogs is almost as good as a young chicken, what a lucky day for me Mmmmm.*" He continued on by calling out to me, "Come on out little dog I am hungry and you don't have a chance of getting away." This looked like for sure that I would not get out of here alive, but I wasn't going to give up I would fight him to my last breath.

"Come on ugly," I said. "You will have a fight on your hands before you have me for dinner."

"I hope you are not as tough as your bragging. I want some nice tender dog meat."

The next thing I knew his paw was on top of my head, he was trying to hold me down. I was able to jerk back far enough that his paw slid off my head, it landed in front of me and I bit down on the tip of his paw with every ounce of strength I could muster up. He yelped in pain, yanked his paw back and slid back a little toward the mouth of the log holding his wounded paw up in the air.

"Tough guy hmm it won't do you any good I've got you cornered, I've got all night, I'll just wait you out and have you for breakfast in the morning."

An hour later I heard a car pull off the highway and come to a screeching stop just outside my log. I could hear people talking. They were lost and looking at a map. They sit there for about 15 minutes; one got out and went into the bushes. When he returned they sped away. Mr. Coyote had backed out of the log when the car stopped. I didn't trust him; he could be just on the outside waiting for me to poke my head out. I crawled as far back in the log as possible and stayed awake the rest of the night. I stayed in the log until the sun was high up in the sky, then I slowly crawled to the mouth of the log and peeked out. There was no coyote in sight. When the car stopped it apparently scared the coyote and he had moved on looking for easier prey. I was safe for now.

I started walking again, my feet were sore from the long walk the day before. It was late in the afternoon before I saw the lights of Tallahassee. I knew that I was on the far side of the city and I had to find my way through it. I was so hungry I had to find something to eat. I came up to a fast food restaurant. "Mm-mmm," I could smell my favorite food, hamburgers. There was a large dog already there trying to turn a trash can over. He looked at me, growled, showed his teeth and said, "Get out of here little mutt this is my territory." I couldn't do anything but watch him as he turned the trash can over. A worker came out the back door of the restaurant about the time that the can hit the ground. I ran and hid under a car. The employee saw the big dog and started chasing him. This was my chance; I ran up to the trash can and found several half eaten hamburgers. What a feast I ate as fast as I could, all the time keeping a weary eye on where the big dog was. I ate so much my belly was hurting. There was still a lot left but I saw the big dog coming back, I grabbed one last burger and carried it with me as I quickly got out of there.

I knew this would be a dangerous night; I had to find a good hiding place. I didn't want a predator or the dog catcher to get me.

Whew! I made it across Interstate 10 with a couple close calls; one driver hollering for me to get out. I still have a long ways to go. I think I know which way is home but am not sure. I might have to circle through the town a few times before I find my way.

It's getting dark and I still don't know what side of town I am on. I'm getting so tired and depressed, wondering if I will ever find my way home. I came upon a big wooded area in the middle of town. Standing at the edge I was looking it over when a cat came up and said, "Hi." She seemed friendly so I said.

"Hi. What is this place?"

"It's a graveyard."

"I need a place to sleep. Is it safe to sleep in there?"

"It should be. There are not many predators in town, you might watch out for hawks." I walked into the woods and into a thicket. This would keep me safe from any hawk.

I woke up the next morning to a line of cars coming into the woods. There was a squirrel on a low limb; so I ask him," What are all those cars doing here?"

He looked down at me and said, "You're not from around here are you?"

I told him I lived just a little ways out of town but had not found my directions home yet.

"This is where humans bury their dead. That line

of cars is for bringing someone out to bury," he informed me.

I started walking again and the first thing that I had to do was find something to eat. A lady sitting on her porch saw me and I heard her say, "O what a cute little dog," I perked up at the compliment, and then she came toward me. I stopped and backed up; I didn't want her to catch me.

"You poor little thing you look hungry." She said. She got up and as she was going in her house she said, "I think I have a left over hamburger, I'll get it for you." I couldn't believe my luck—my favorite food. But I was not going to let her catch me. When she came out and sat the hamburger down I backed up away from her.

"Poor thing," she said. "You must be afraid." She walked out in the yard and sat the bowl down with the hamburger in it. When she got back on the porch I eased up and kept my eye on her as I quickly ate the delicious hamburger. When I finished I took off down the sidewalk in a fast run.

I was afraid this would be another day of searching all over town. I came up on a large street and heard a taxi driver tell his passenger that they were on Monroe. I vaguely remember Calvin talking about Monroe Street. I crossed it and there was Florida State Campus. I had been on campus with Calvin but not in this area. I walked a few more block, rounded a corner and jumped for joy. I couldn't believe my eyes, there it was. Bryan Hall, the building where Calvin works. I ran to the building. Calvin had brought me here, a couple times. It was so wonderful to find a place that I recognized; I sat and just gazed at the building for a good 10 minutes. Finally—I knew my way home.

I still had a long ways to go, but now I was quite sure that I know the right road to take out of Tallahassee. The first sign I would look for when I did get out of town would be the airport and after that I would be traveling in a dangerous area again.

It wasn't long until I was outside the city limits. It was very noisy as I passed the runway. An airplane, with a loud whining noise, came in for landing about 50 feet over my head and it about scared me to death.

I was tired, but I was determined to walk as fast as I could, hoping to get home before dark. An hour later it started getting dark and I still was not home. It would be dangerous but I decided to keep going as long as I could. There was no moon and soon it was so dark I could hardly see the road. I heard the distinctive howl of a coyote and he was very close to me. I had no protection out here and I could not out run him. From a distance he saw me; my ugly white coat gave me away. He was coming at me full speed, I had no choice but to run as fast as I could and try to hide from him. He was laughing because he was sure he could catch me. I rounded a bend in the road and there was a house with the porch light on. I headed for it as fast as my little legs would carry me.

I could see a large dog in the yard, and hoped he was friendly. He spotted me and came at me in a dead run. Here I was caught between a coyote and a large mean looking dog. I give up, this is surely the end, I have walked all this way just to get caught a couple miles from my safe home. I laid down and closed my eyes hoping it would all be over quickly. I could hear the dog coming up fast from the front of me and the coyote coming up to my rear. The dog was the closest and would probably get to me first. I opened my eyes to watch, then shut them fast again as he was almost on me. I didn't feel him hit me so I opened my eyes again. He made his jump, I shut my eyes once more, felt nothing then opened them again as he sailed over my head and attacked the coyote that was about to nab me. What luck, he was not after me but was after the coyote.

After running the coyote off into the woods, he came back and said, "Little girl what are you doing out here in this God forsaken place at this hour?"

All I could say was, "Thank you, thank you." After I got my wind back I said, "I'm heading home I live a couple miles down the road on the dirt lane."

His name was JD, and he said, "I knew the way to the dirt lane. The dirt lane has become the center of all the talk among animals around here; I hear there have been a lot of things happening there."

"Yes, the dirt lane has become famous, there has been too much happening there."

We went to his house and sat on the porch while I rested for an hour. I told him about the accident and my journey back home. "What a great guy!" He walked with me the final two miles to my house. I told him about my life and about all the nice animals that lived on the dirt lane. He said, "Maybe I will come and visit sometime."

"You are more than welcome anytime," I said and meant it.

After thanking JD again I bid him good-bye. It was just before daybreak when I went through my doggie door and into the bedroom where Calvin was. I was so tired I couldn't jump up on the bed; all I could do was let out a whine. Calvin jumped up in the dark and started hollering, "Ms Kelly is that you?" He finally got to a light switch and turned it on.

He had a leg and arm in casts from the accident. He still found the strength to pick me up and hug me. What a wonderful reunion. It feels great to be back to my good home and knowing that Calvin had survived the wreck. The next day Calvin took me to the vet and they checked me over. Then they brought out a needle and put a tattoo on my ear. I heard Calvin tell the vet, "I hope this will keep me from losing her again." They had tattooed a number on my ear so if I got lost again Calvin could easily find me.

College spring term is out and it is a repeat of prior years, students dumping their pets in our area. Calvin had two dogs, two cats and a white rabbit to show up in his yard. He picked up the rabbit first because dog and cats love to eat rabbits. He had an empty bird cage so he placed the rabbit in it. One of the dogs was a large German Shepherd and the other a mixed breed, a little larger than me. The German Shepherd named Hercules had been a house dog for the four years his master was in college. I told him that Calvin would not let him stay in the house, but he could stay on the screened back porch.

The mixed breed dog, Ben was also a house dog. I told him, "I didn't know if Calvin is going to keep you, Hercules, or neither one of you, if he doesn't he will find good homes for both of you." I told the cats they were in the same predicament, "A good home will be found."

The spring moved into summer and we didn't get anymore unwanted animals from the college. Calvin found homes for all the animals that had been dumped except Hercules; he decided to keep him for an extra watch dog.

The woman that wanted the cats asked if she could also have Win. "Sure," Calvin replied, "I have two other cats and that is enough for me." Too bad that Calvin didn't keep the new cats and give her Lin and Kim.

It was a hot August day and we were staying on the porch where it was a little cooler. A large male raccoon came out of the forest and was moaning and slobbering. He was bumping into everything and would try to bite what ever he bumped into.

Tuff Boy hollered to me from the top of a tree. "Ms Kelly that raccoon has rabies and you need to get in the house." I ask him what rabies was and he said that it was a disease that if any animal didn't have a shot to protect them can easily get the disease from an infected animal. The disease is deadly and extremely contagious, even humans can catch the disease if bitten.

"Tell Lin, and Kim to get on the roof, the disease

will make the raccoon go blind if it hasn't alread. They should be safe up there."

Calvin came home from work about the time all the commotion started. He immediately knew what was wrong with the raccoon and ran in the house and came out with his shotgun. There was only one thing that Calvin could do to keep the disease from being spread to other animals and that was to put the raccoon out of its misery, so he shot him.

He called Animal Control to come and pick up the dead raccoon. They would have to dispose of it to keep the disease from spreading. Calvin brought out some kerosene and burned the area where the raccoon fell, this would kill any of the disease that was in the soil.

I thought I knew everything about predators and danger but realized I still have a lot to learn. This disease comes around in the heat of summer, usually in August. There are a lot of wild animals besides dogs, cats and humans that can contact it.

Red has to teach Hercules everything. He had always been a house pet and now he would have to change to a farm watch dog. He wasn't afraid of anything and Red figured he would be easily trained. The first time Red spotted a coyote close to the yard he showed him to Hercules. When the coyote saw Hercules he turned around and ran. Hercules is a big guy much bigger than Red. I sure was happy that he was my friend.

Red and I took Hercules around to the neighborhood so he could meet all the animals. Everyone welcomed him to the dirt lane neighborhood. They knew he would be a great protector against predators. Just the sight of him walking around would deter a lot of them from trying to attack.

CHAPTER FIVE

Summer arrived and things were a little better, the feud had died down. Kim and Lin were still in their own world and kept their normal distance from us. The back porch was a gathering place for Red, Suzie, Hercules, me and other farm animal that wanted to come in for a while. I still had the doggie door into the house from the back porch which was very convenient for me.

When Florida State's spring semester ended we had pets dumped on the dirt lane again. Animal Control had wised up and were there waiting to pick them up. But they missed one tiny yellow kitten that showed up at the house. No one saw it until it climbed on the side porch and began crying. I couldn't believe my eyes; Kim and Lin took the little tyke in and were mothering him. There is a little humanity in those two mean cats after all. It looked like they just might come around to being peaceful. They named the kitten Jim Bob and called him JB.

JB was a cute little guy and we let him play in the yard. Kim and Lin would come out to watch him. We would not bother them hoping they would get to the point where we could all live in peace.

I helped teach JB about all the predators that would come out of the National Forest and get him if he didn't keep his guard up. Since he was the only young guy on the place everybody played with him and protected him. He was getting spoiled with all the attention he was getting.

Sometimes Calvin had to go out of town on a business trip and Raymond his next door neighbor would look after me and the rest of Calvin's animals and property. Raymond would come over at night and make sure I was in bed, then come back over the next morning to check on me. He worked nights as guard and his house being just across the dirt lane, during the day he could watch Calvin's place and be working in his yard at the same time. He was a nice and caring neighbor.

I liked Raymond. He was a nice person but I had rather stay at home than at his house. This arrangement that Raymond and Calvin had for me while he was gone suited me just fine. The only thing sometimes I would get mad if Calvin was gone for a long time. A couple times I left my scent on his bed, just to let him know he was staying away too long. He never got mad and quickly figured out why I did that.

When he came home he would tell me I was bad but I would look as pitiful as I could and he would feel guilty for leaving me so long and would take me to town for my favorite treat, a big delicious juicy hamburger.

Early one morning there was a loud commotion in the bird pen. Red, Suzie, Hercules, and I ran out to see what the racket was all about. When we got to the gate an old granddad Pigeon told us that there was a chicken snake in their pen. He had got through a small opening in a rotten board in the wall of the old barn. He was trying to get up in the loft where the eggs and baby birds were. Calvin wasn't home so we had to figure out a way to get the snake out. I could show Red how to open the bird pen gate but neither one of us could climb up in the barn loft.

We ran back to the house and I asked Kim to help us get the snake out of the barn, we assured her that it was not poisonous.

"That is your problems not mine," was her snotty reply.

"You always want us to guard JB against predators, that is not our problem but we help you out by taking care of him," Red replied, "So it is time you help us for a change."

"Ok! I'll help you." Kim quickly answered, she was afraid we would quit helping them look after JB.

We ran back to the pen knowing that the snake would be getting close to the babies or eggs. I showed Red how to open the gate and in two jumps he had it open. We rushed into the barn. I was afraid that we were too late, the snake was close to a nest of baby fan tail pigeons high up in the barn loft.

Jerome the male pigeon made a dive at the snake and stopped him for a moment. Kim started climbing toward the snake. The snake saw her coming and tried again to get to the nest of baby pigeons. He was so close I thought for sure he was going to get one of them. Bravely, Jerome and his mate Rachel both dived and pecked him on the top of his head. They were able to keep him at bay until Kim got up in the loft. When the snake saw Kim closing in on him he gave up and quickly departed through the hole he came in through.

After we got the snake run out, Red and I were able to drag up a small limb and poke it in the hole so no more snakes could get through until we could alert Calvin about the hole and he would fix it permanently.

We thanked Kim for her help and explained to her, "See how we can help each other, if you and Lin would only cooperate with us we could have a much safer and peaceful place to live." She was still aloof from us and replied in a mocking swagger, "Yes, sure."

JB was now six months old and quite a handsome young tomcat. He was coming of age and was strutting about showing off. I am afraid we spoiled him because he become arrogant and impossible to deal with. At night he would prowl around and staying up late. Kim and Lin were very worried about him and pleaded with, Red, Suzie and me to watch after him. We told them we would do the best we could.

It wasn't long until he was staying out all night and sometimes would come home in the early morning all cut up from having a fight with another tomcat.

At one year old he was the biggest tomcat living on the dirt lane. Ever since he was a tiny kitten and had found his way to the side porch he has received the best of care and plenty of exercise. Calvin had taken him to the vet for a check up shortly after he arrived. He had the best nutritional food money could buy. Living outside all his life had also toughened him up. Most cats on the dirt lane were house cats and didn't get enough exercise so they were soft and weak. JB's hair was slick and shiny and he had large hard muscles.

When he was near two years old, he came in early one morning, after being out all night. "I have been in a fight with the meanest and toughest tomcat. He was the ruler over all cats on the dirt lane, and I whipped him good and made him run for his life. Now I am number one and will rule over every cat that lives on or near the dirt lane. I plan on changing a lot of things, and I will make sure that each and everyone knows that I am the boss."

After winning the fight he changed. With his new power he became rude and mean. We heard rumors that he was picking on everyone that lived on the dirt lane, not only all the cats but every small animal that he could beat up. It wasn't long until everyone on the dirt lane hated him and avoided any contact with him. Lin asked," What did I do wrong?" Tuff Boy said, "What went wrong was he took after your ways, mean as a snake and ornery as a mule." Tuff Boys comment went right over her head and she had no idea that he was talking about her.

A couple months after JB became king of the dirt lane he got mad at Sally, and clawed her up. Raymond decided he had enough; it was time something was done about JB. Calvin agreed with him and they called the Animal Control. They said," We will come out and pick him up. There are a lot of folks looking for a cat—even mean ones; many businesses need cats to keep down the population of mice and rats." Raymond and Calvin agreed and told them to come pick him up as soon as possible.

JB had wised up about Animal Control; he had seen others picked up by them. They were going to have a hard time getting him. He was a smart cat and knew how to hide in the woods.

It had been six months since Raymond and Calvin had called Animal Control on JB. They had tried and tried to catch him but he was always able to give them the slip. The other animals on the dirt lane were sick and tired of him and were all saying, "We have to do something about him." A meeting was called for all interested animals about helping Animal Control catch JB. The meeting was held on Calvin's back porch. There was a large crowd that attended. Everyone had ideas on how to get him caught. It was decided during the day from sun up till sun down someone would be on duty to watch JB and keep up with where he was. When the Animal Control came out, whoever was following JB would give a signal and others would join him when the Animal Control saw a gathering of several animals they would investigate.

JB found out what was going on but there was nothing he could do about it since everyone was against him. They told him, "You can only rule by force when the majority allows you. Since you feel that you are an all powerful dictator and can do whatever you want disregarding the feelings of others, have caused you to lose our respect. It is time that you left the dirt lane forever. You are not our leader anymore." He realized that he was in a corner and begged them to help him fight off the Animal Control and he would change his ways. There was a vote taken in secret and he lost. We told him that he had to go. He got mad and said, "They will never catch me, and everyone of you had better watch out and keep clear of me."

It wasn't long after that when the Animal Control came out to the dirt lane, all the cats followed right behind JB until the man could run him down and catch him. Everyone rejoiced as Animal Control put him in the truck and headed back to Tallahassee. We could hear him as the truck pulled away hollering, "I will be back and I will get all of you for what you have done, mark my word—each and everyone of you will pay dearly for this." He didn't scare anyone; they knew he was finally gone for good. There was a celebration on the dirt lane everyone was dancing and singing in relief. I was sorry that JB turned out the way he did. Sometimes there is no control over young ones, when they turn bad they have to pay the price.

Peace came back to the dirt lane. This time there was a committee selected to vote on the next ruler and laid down laws that he must follow. They made sure that no one would have all the power again.

Suzie began to have health problems. Calvin took her to the vet and he said that her hearing was getting bad. "She can still play with us outside," Red said. "We will watch out for predators for her since she will have a problem hearing them. It won't take predators long to realize she can't hear and will slip up on her back." I would go down to Mary's house and visit with Suzie. She looked very sick. Red and I stayed by her side everyday all day long. We would take her for walks in the yard and play what little we could. She looked so sad and I felt awful for the condition she was getting in. She was getting up in years and began to have all kind of health problems, arthritis, swelling in her paws and heart trouble. Calvin was taking her to the vet most every week. I was with him the last time he took her, the vet said that he had done all he could for her. "Just take her home and let her live out the rest of her life the best that she can." He instructed.

Six months after Suzie went deaf she started losing her eye sight. Red and I would have to get on each side of her so she could feel our prescience when we were out in the yard. It wasn't long until she lost all her sight and hearing. Mary had to carry her outside to potty. I felt so sorry for her; she was such a good dog and mother to all her many puppies. We could not even talk to her anymore. All Red and I could do was watch and help the best we could when Mary brought her out to potty.

Everyday I could see that Suzie's health was getting worse. This is a sad time for everyone; Suzie was loved and respected by all the animals on the dirt lane. Not long after she went blind, Mary came up to the house and told Calvin that Suzie had died in her sleep. I felt so bad. Three of my best friends are now in doggie heaven. It would take me a long time to get over her death. Calvin buried her beside John Henry.

Another change in my life, Ron and Mary were moving, they were expecting another baby and the mobile home was not big enough for a family of five. Mary said that Red was such a good protector for her girls she just had to have him. Calvin said, with a sad look at Red, "Ok you can take him, but Ms Kelly and I will want to visit him sometimes." Red was happy. He licked my face and said good-bye as they loaded up and barked as they drove down the dirt lane. I ran down the dirt lane behind them and watched the car until it turned on the gravel road. I turned and slowly, with my head down, walked back to the house. I don't know what I was going to do with out my best friend Red.

Now it was just me, Hercules and the cats. I would really have to watch my back while out playing. They had come around a lot, but with Red gone they may go back to their old ways. Hercules is good but didn't understand or know how to control the cats like Red did.

Since everyone had moved out, Calvin decided to move into the cabin and rent out the house. I hope who ever rents it will have a dog or two. Without any help those cats have begun driving me crazy. They are doing just what I was afraid they would do; they went back to their old mean hateful ways.

I supervised Calvin's move to the cabin, it was small and a lot of things that wouldn't fit was taken to town and given to the Salvation Army. That meant that I got to ride to town everyday. It was fun getting to go to town. We were in a section of Tallahassee that I never knew existed. I was able to learn about another side of town besides the University, Capitol buildings and the road to Georgia.

When we headed toward home and turned in on the dirt lane Calvin would let me sit on his lap with my head out the window and the wind hitting me in the face. I am so happy to be living with Calvin. I have learned a lot about living in the country and have many good friends. What a wonderful life I am having.

We got settled in the cabin and I got to sleep in bed with Calvin on my own pillow. While he was at work I would play outside and there was always food and a day bed on the porch for me to take a nap during the day. I didn't have to bother with the cats except their teasing because the house was across the yard from the cabin.

Lin and Kim had nothing to do but aggravate me. They would holler from the porch, "Hey Ms Kelly you are the ugliest apricot poodle. I never saw a white and red spotted apricot poodle. Is that a new breed of ugly dogs? You need to enter the yearly contest for the ugliest dog, you would win hands down." Then they both would roll around on the porch laughing until their sides began to hurt. I thought they were going to come around when we let them in the yard and even protected JB for them. Since all my support is gone they have really ganged up on me.

Lately they expanded their territory and now they are claiming the yard. There is nothing I can do but stay close to the cabin so I can scoot through the doggie door to the screened in porch. They can not get me here but will stand just outside and dare me to come out. Poor old Hercules he just didn't know how to keep Lin and Kim under control. They are just too smart for him and they were about to drive him crazy. Hercules was always just a house dog, he now lived on the old back porch where Suzie stayed and I rarely see him. He just lays around on the porch all day and sleeps. Lin will say, "Hey ugly come on out and play, we love spotted Apricot Poodle, what ever that is. I know if Lin wasn't so mean I could make friends with Kim. She is afraid of her sister and will go along with her nasty ways.

Calvin expanded the side porch and screened it in. I was hoping that he would make those mean cats move, but he put in a small cat door in where they could go in and out as they pleased. They had to do a lot of bragging about their new digs.

A month after we moved to the cabin, Calvin had an advertisement put in the Tallahassee paper advertising the house for rent. It was two weeks later when he had two different people wanting to rent it. Calvin didn't have everything out of the house at that time. He said it would be another month or two before he would rent it out.

When Calvin was home he was always busy outside getting everything ready for the renter. We moved stuff to the tool shed, planted some shrubbery in the yard, trimmed the trees and bushes. The biggest project was painting the house and making sure that the roof was leak-proof. It was fun being by Calvin's side while he worked. I didn't have to worry about the cats when Calvin was with me. They were meek as lambs and was afraid to tease me.

It was a couple months later when a single grandmother came, looked at the house and wanted to rent it. Calvin still didn't have everything out of the house.

The lady, Martha, said that she had been transferred to Tallahassee and needed a place right away. She said she had a friend in town that she could stay with for a week or so.

"I will start putting my stuff on the side porch," Calvin told her. "I just increased the size of it and screened it in and I should be able to have all my stuff out of the house and on the porch in a few days. In the meantime you can start putting your stuff on the back porch and move in to each room as I move out."

It was just a week later when Calvin had most of his stuff on the side porch and Margie had her stuff on the back porch and Calvin took me to town for my favorite treat, a juicy hamburger. When we returned home and rounded the last curve in the dirt lane we both were horrified!! The yard was full of people and the house was burning down.

The renter was running around in the yard screaming!! I heard her tell Calvin that she had a skillet of meat on the kitchen stove cooking and had gone into the back bedroom with her grandchildren and when she returned to the kitchen it was on fire. She had to get her grandchildren out of the house first. One of them was so scared he ran back in. When she got him out the second time it was too late, the house being an old wooden building went up in flames fast.

This was a huge loss for Calvin. The rent from the house was going to be a big part of his retirement. He was devastated over his loss. He had lived in the house for 22 years and for several days after the fire he would sit in the yard and look at his destroyed home.

Hercules moved under the cabin. He had plenty room to get under it and Calvin made him a nice bed. Since the cats didn't have their porch anymore, Calvin fixed them a place in the storage shed so they could go in and out. This put them way back to the rear edge of the yard, next to the two acres of woods. At least they were out of my hair.

Now I had the upper hand and would go out in the yard and yell, "Hey you mean ugly cats how do you like your new home? Looks like you all are back living in the ghetto. At least it is much better than the trashy mobile home you all were born under. I believe that I heard somewhere that anyone living in or under a rundown mobile home is called trailer trash. Is that what you two are Trailer Trash?" It felt so good to get back at them for all the misery they had dished out to me with their constant teasing.

Since the house is gone, Calvin decided to retire, sell the cabin and four acres and move to Miami, Florida. His cousin, Adrian that he was raised with asked him to share a condo with him and his daughter Pam. Calvin sent Adrian the money for his half of the condo.

Moving into a big city and living in a condo is going to be a much different life than what I have enjoyed here on this little farm. I am already wondering what my new life will be like.

We had a lot of stuff in the storage sheds and what didn't sell was given away. Once again, we took daily trips to the Salvation Army. As usual, I was enjoying every trip. I knew each night we would stop and have hamburgers during our deliveries.

Calvin had the place up for sale for over a month and had a lot of people looking at it but got no offers.

Finally, after another month of waiting, a couple came out to look and were very interested in buying. They also wanted all the animals that were left. There was a day of negotiation, a price was agreed on and the place was sold.

Kim and Lin would still have a home. They were so happy they quit bothering me and became very nice. "I know we have never gotten along and I am sorry for all we have done to you. If it was to do over I think we could be friends," Kim said.

The buyers of the property were happy to get Hercules for a watch dog.

I knew that Miami was over five hundred miles away and it was going to be a long and hard trip. To be honest, I was dreading the long ride and the fact that we were going to start all over again. I loved my life and all my adventures in Tallahassee. I will miss the animals on the dirt lane. I went around and visited all of them for the last time. They were sad to see me go. I told them to keep up the good work in controlling any animal that would try to come on the dirt lane and be a dictator.

Finally the day came, Calvin had loaded up the van and he had fixed me a pillow next to him. Every crack and corner of the van was full of stuff with just enough room for me to sit on top of a pillow and for Calvin to have room to drive. We left the cabin without looking back. As we neared the end of the dirt lane I began to remember all the good and bad times I had on this old worn out road. We came to the gravel road and I then turned and looked back down the dirt lane for the last time. I looked at Calvin and knew he wanted to look back but couldn't. I could see that his eyes were watering and I knew he was already missing his old home. But, it was gone now and we had to look to the future.

On our way out of Tallahassee, Calvin took me to work with him. This would be his last day to work after this day he would be retired. He took me around to all his employees and co-workers. It was fun, everyone wanted to pet me and tell me how cute I am. I'm just glad that they did not know that I was supposed to be apricot in color. They even thought the four spots on my body that had turned apricot color from the coyote's bite, were cute. I was eating up all this attention. If my mean brothers could only see me now. I know they would be jealous of all that I have accomplished. We spent a couple hours at his work, then Calvin made his last round and said good-bye to each and everyone and they all had to give me a little hug and pat.

We headed out of the financial aid office, down the elevator and outside. Calvin stopped, turned and for a few minutes looked at the building. This was the Seminole football stadium; Calvin had worked here ever since offices had been built around it. After a couple minutes walking around on the ground, we loaded up in the van and headed out of Tallahassee. As we left the city limits I was glued to the window, this is territory that I had never seen or couldn't remember.

We had only traveled for an hour when Calvin surprised me and stopped at the puppy mill where I was born. He was showing me off to Margie and she kept saying how nice I looked but I didn't believe her, I still remember her putting me in the closet when prospective show dog buyers came shopping. I decided to walk around on my own and visit all the dogs. To my surprise my mother and dad were there.

Dad said after he retired, his owner paid for him and mother, for the rest of their lives to live here and have the best of food and medical attention.

Their pen is very large and they have a doggy door and the run of the place. I was so sad my parents are getting up in years.

"What is your name now honey?" My dad asked.

"It's Ms Kelly and I love it," I exclaimed excitedly.

"Ms Kelly how did you learn the human language so well?"

"I listened not only to their voice but their body language. It was easy and I now know the language of a lot of animals too. I know the language of doves, wild and tame, pigeons, chickens, geese, peacocks, guinea fowl, squirrels and many more other animals then I can remember. Living out of town on the little farm gave me the chance to meet and learn from a lot of different animals and birds. There are no city dogs or show dogs that had the opportunities that I have had while living out in the country."

"Remember when you were a little puppy," dad said. "I told you that you were smarter and would go a long way, much more than your brothers? It sounds like you have had a much better and happier life than they have. I am so proud of you. Your brothers have no talent and even if they succeed in show business it will not last long and when they are too old for the show business they will have nowhere to go. It is very hard for an older dog to find a good home."

I told mother and dad that Calvin had entered me in a dog mutt race and I won the race and got the trophy. I told them what fun I had when Calvin and I entered the winning circle. "I can still hear the crowd clapping and congratulating me on my win!" I explained to them.

"You are the smartest and nicest child I have ever had. I am so proud of you. Winning the mutt race alone was much more than anything your brothers accomplished."

Dad really made me feel good and it was hard to bid my parents good-bye knowing I would probably never see them again.

We pulled out of the driveway, turned the van toward Miami and a new life.

I was already wondering what kind of adventures I would have in the city of Miami.

MY LAST VIEW OF THE FAMOUS DIRT LANE

—COMING SOON—

ADVENTURES OF MS KELLY IN MIAMI